TABLE OF CONTENTS

ACRONYMS

1ID	1st Infantry Division
AIT	Army Information Team
AAH	Asaib Ahl al-Haq
AOR	Area of Responsibility
BATT	British Army Training Team
CAT	Civil Action Team
COIN	Counterinsurgency
DGDP	Directorate of Graduate Degree Programs
DLF	Dhofari Liberation Front
EW	Electronic Warfare
GDP	Graduate Degree Programs
IIA	Inform and Influence Activities
IO	Information Operations
ISF	Iraqi Security Forces
JAM	Jaysh al-Mahdi
KH	Kata'ib Hezbollah
KLE	Key Leader Engagement
LOE	Line of Effort
MILDEC	Military Deception
OPSEC	Operational Security
ORSA	Operations Research and Systems Analysis
PAO	Public Affairs Office
PDB	Promised Day Brigade

PFLO	Popular Front for the Liberation of Oman
PFLOAG	Popular Front for the Liberation of Oman and the Arabian Gulf
PRT	Provincial Reconstruction Team
PSYOP	Psychological Operations
SAS	Special Air Service
SEG	Shia Extremist Group
SGA	Small Group Advisor
SIAM	Southern Iraq Assessment Model
USD-S	United States Division-South
USF-I	United States Forces-Iraq
VEN	Violent Extremist Network

ILLUSTRATIONS

CHAPTER 1

INTRODUCTION

Information Operations and conflict

The concept of information operations (IO) is over thirty years old, yet US Army professionals continue to debate what its purpose is, whether or not information operations are relevant, and if so, how it should be integrated into military operations. Military theorists have written about the requirement to control information in conflict, expressing their viewpoints through the context of the conflicts in which they were involved and calling IO by other names such as propaganda or information services. Yet inconsistencies in terms and military professionals not understanding how the context of a conflict determines the ways in which IO are to be integrated into larger campaign strategies hinder a clear understanding of the concept.

Information operations are concerned with the control and manipulation of information. The discipline evolved from a technical approach to command and control targeting and broadened to include the application of non-technical capabilities in order to have effects that are influential both within and outside of a conflict's theater of operations. Integration of IO is dependent upon the type of conflict in which the military is involved. This thesis examines the integration of information into US Army operations during periods of unstable peace and insurgency, and suggests that IO may be integrated in four general ways: the control of information both leaving the conflict and within, the manipulation of information to have an effect upon adversarial target audiences and decision makers, and to protect operations.

1

Research Questions

This thesis seeks to answer the following generic research question: what is the role of information within conflict? To answer this question, the thesis will address three supporting questions.

1. How important is adaptability in designing a campaign strategy?

2. What is the relationship between security operations, civil capacity operations, and the information environment?

3. What is the relationship between information and the convergent nature of conflict?

Methodology

This study is based upon a close examination of military theorists' principles, US Army doctrine, and historical case studies. Review of selected military theorists' writings and the IO doctrinal evolution will be used to create the case study analytical framework. The historical analysis of the British Army in Dhofar, 1970-1975, and the 1st Infantry Division in Southern Iraq, 2010-2011, will be conducted using a combination of archival research and primary source interviews of commanders and participants of the relevant case studies. Each case study will examine the respective organization's strategies and operations and identify any lessons learned.

Chapter 2 examines the theories and principle of selected military theorists and creates three analytical constructs to be applied to the case studies. Chapter 3 reviews the doctrinal evolution of information operations in order to provide a basic understanding of the discipline and provide in greater detail the four ways of integration into military operations.

The Dhofar counterinsurgency is reviewed in Chapter 4. Dhofar is unique in the sense that the Dhofari Information Service created as part of the Watts Plan[1] performed many of the same tasks that have been performed by information operations in more recent conflicts, years before the concept was created by the United States. The actions of the 1st Infantry Division in southern Iraq, 2010 to 2011, are examined in chapter 5 to illustrate how IO have been integrated during a more contemporary conflict. Chapter 6 provides the conclusions of the case studies and on the integration of IO, and provides recommendations for future research as well as advice for future commanders and practitioners.

Summary of Results

The historical record, the ideas of relevant military theorists, and US Army doctrine support the premise that information is integral to US Army operations during conflict. Information operations are a means for controlling and manipulating information in support of government forces objectives. The integration of IO into military operations is contextually dependent upon the conflict in which IO is being applied. Similar, general ways are common to most conflicts, yet the specific ways of integration are dependent upon the unique contexts of each conflict. The error would be in a military unit applying IO without thoroughly understanding the conflict in which it is involved.

---

[1]Discussion of the Watts Plan will be discussed in chapter 4.

CHAPTER 2

MILITARY THEORISTS REVIEW

The counterinsurgency (COIN) principles of selected military theorists must be reviewed in order to establish the analytical framework of analysis to be applied to the subsequent case studies of this thesis.[2] The military theorists selected for review are General Sir Frank Edward Kitson, Sir Robert Thompson, Colonel John McCuen, Lieutenant Colonel David Galula, and Lieutenant Colonel (retired) Frank Hoffman.[3] The context of the analytical constructs that will be used to conduct the Dhofar and Iraq case studies will be established using their principles and theories.

Three analytical constructs are to be applied to the case studies. The first construct is the requirement that leaders (both civilian and military) and campaign planners be adaptable when organizing for, planning, and executing their operations' strategies. The second construct is that leaders and campaign planners understand the relationship between security civil capacity operations, and the information environment. The final

---

[2]The author is deliberately avoiding identifying the military theorists as 'COIN' theorist, though their principles are derived from the counterinsurgency conflicts in which they participated. The author has observed a tendency within the US Army to regard insurgency, and other forms of conflict, as separate from 'war'. The current doctrinal spectrum of warfare provides a counter to this perspective and defines conflict along a continuum that includes insurgency and general war as forms of conflict that are capable of rapidly transitioning from one to the other. The current doctrinal spectrum of warfare will be examined later in this chapter. For clarity, within this thesis the author uses the term conflict to apply to all forms of warfare, and specifically addresses unstable peace and insurgency in the following discussion.

[3]Biographical data for each will be provided later in the chapter.

construct is that leaders and campaign planners understand the convergent nature of conflict.[4]

Introduction of the military theorists

General Sir Frank Edward Kitson was a British officer who participated in many counterinsurgency campaigns.[5] He wrote extensively on low intensity and counterinsurgent warfare, his works including *Gangs and Counter-gangs* (1960), *Low Intensity Operations: Subversion, Insurgency and Peacekeeping* (1971), and *Bunch of Five* (1977). *Bunch of Five* is a collection of five case studies of conflicts Kitson was personally involved with and is the source of those principles of his examined in this chapter. Kitson frequently referred to the use of propaganda and the need to win the minds of men.[6]

Sir Robert Thompson was a British Royal Air Force officer who served during the Malayan Emergency in the 1950s and as head of the British Advisory Mission during the Vietnam War. He wrote extensively about counterinsurgent warfare; his works included books, journal and newspaper articles, and his book *Defeating Communist Insurgency*

---

[4]The explanation of the three constructs is the purpose of this chapter; explanation of each follows. Also, the author has avoided the use of the terms and phrases counterinsurgent, counterinsurgency planner, insurgent and counterinsurgent leader intentionally in order to avoid focusing this chapter solely on counterinsurgency warfare. The author believes the three constructs are applicable to all forms of conflict, not solely insurgencies. The term 'adversary' will be used in place of insurgent when applicable.

[5]Kitson's campaigns include the Mau Mau Uprising in Kenya, the Malayan Emergency, the Omani insurgencies of the 1950s, Cyprus, and Northern Ireland.

[6]Frank Kitson, *Bunch of Five* (London: Faber and Faber, 1977). Author's analysis of Kitson's principles; the principles will be examined in greater detail later in the chapter.

provides the counterinsurgency principles of his examined in this chapter. Thompson, with principles similar to Kitson's, reinforced the use of propaganda to protect the legitimacy of the government and implied that the key terrain during an insurgency was the minds of the people. His principles emphasized the need for a clear political end state and a plan enabled by integrated civil and military action.[7]

Lieutenant Colonel David Galula was a French Army officer who studied and fought in irregular wars in China, Greece, Indochina, and Algeria. He collected his experiences from Algeria into his books *Counterinsurgency Warfare: Theory and Practice* and *Pacification in Algeria: 1956-1958*. His writings have three core observations: the counterinsurgent must conduct a thorough analysis of the conflict they are in and organize appropriately; the population is the primary target; and insurgent warfare is a fight for the minds of men.[8] In addition to the principles that Galula provided, he also described the context of insurgent warfare by providing causes for insurgencies, the roles of nationalism and communism within the conflicts, and the linkage between the political leadership and the campaign strategy.[9]

Colonel John McCuen was a US Army officer who served during the Vietnam War. His experiences were collected in his book *The Art of Counter-Revolutionary War*,

---

[7]Robert Thompson, *Defeating Communist Insurgency* (London: Chatto and Windus, 1966). Author's summary of Thompson's principles; the principles will be presented in greater detail later in this chapter.

[8]Mao heavily influenced Galula from the perspective of focusing on the population instead of terrain during counterinsurgent operations.

[9]David Galula, *Counterinsurgency Warfare, Theory and Practice* (Westport, CT: Praeger Security International, 2006). Author's analysis of Galula's principles; his principles will be examined in greater detail later in this chapter.

which provides those principles of his examined in this chapter. McCuen maintained

close ties to the US Army after his retirement and continued to write on the nature of

current and future warfare until his death in 2010.[10] McCuen's principles focused on the

population, implied the need for an aggressive propaganda element, and stressed the

requirement of unified action between both civilian and military agencies. His latter

work, specifically "Hybrid Wars" printed in *Military Review*, March-April 2008,

addressed the convergent nature of conflict.[11]

Lieutenant Colonel (Retired) Frank Hoffman is a retired US Marine Corps officer.

As of June 20, 2011 he has served at the National Defense University as a Senior

Research Fellow with the Institute for National Strategic Studies. His experiences include

serving as an analyst and advisor to the Marine Corps, studying emerging hybrid threats

and asymmetric warfare concepts, and contributing to the writing of the US Army/Marine

Corps counterinsurgency manual.[12] He has written extensively about current threats, and

---

[10]McCuen had a varied post-Army career; in addition to being a prolific writer on counter-insurgency and asymmetric warfare, he served as a guest lecturer for military audiences and as General Dynamics Chief of Abrams Tanks Training. This is not a complete listing of his post-Army employment.

[11]John J. McCuen, *The Art of Counter-Revolutionary War* (Harrisburg, PA: Stockpole Books, 1966); John J. McCuen, "Hybrid Wars," *Military Review* (March-April 2008): 107-113. Discussion of McCuen's principles and the subject of "Hybrid Wars" will be examined in greater detail later in this chapter. McCuen is noteworthy within the context of this chapter in that he continued to be active in discussions on the nature of conflict until his death in 2010, and focused attention to the physical and conceptual dimensions of conflict, expressed through his contributions to the 'hybrid warfare' debate. Thompson, Kitson, and Galula also expressed this concept through their suggested applications of propaganda to counterinsurgent strategies.

[12]Foreign Policy Research Institute, http://www.fpri.org/about/people/ hoffman.html (accessed November 6, 2011).

his observations on hybrid warfare, along with McCuen's, provide the basis of this chapter's discussion pertaining to the convergent nature of conflict analytical construct.

Analytical construct one: Adaptability

An adversary, during periods of unstable peace and insurgency, will employ unconventional means against government forces. Therefore, it is implied that the government be adaptable when designing its strategy. Adaptability by government forces is exercised through understanding the context of the conflict and applying that understanding to campaign objectives, the task organization of government forces, and how they anticipate and respond to events occurring within the conflict.

Understanding the context of a conflict is expressed across the broader context of the 'the spectrum of conflict', understanding the causes of conflict, and knowing the adversarial forces.[13] Current US Army doctrine defines the spectrum of conflict as an ascending scale of violence ranging across four broad categories: stable peace, unstable peace, insurgency, and general war.[14]

Stable peace is the absence of militarily significant violence. Actors limit activities to peaceful interaction, which may include intense competition, cooperation,

---

[13]Department of the Army, Field Manual (FM) 3-0, *Operations,* change 1 (Washington, DC: Government Printing Office, February 2008), 2-1. This chapter will examine the causes of conflict expressed through an insurgency perspective. Knowing the adversarial forces goes beyond force strengths and weapon capabilities to include knowing which areas are controlled by adversaries and their relationships to the population.

[14]Ibid.

and assistance. Tensions exist, but all parties recognize that they may achieve their interests through means other than violence.[15]

Unstable peace is when one or more parties threaten or use violence to accomplish their objectives. It may also be the period after violent conflict has occurred, and when interventionist powers may be asked to apply force to enable peace operations.[16]

Insurgency, as defined by FM 3-0, *Operations*, is the "organized movement of subversion and violence by a group or movement that seeks to overthrow or force change of a governing authority."[17] It is interstate and intrastate conflict short of combined arms maneuver by conventional forces, and may occur in the aftermath of general war, the degeneration of unstable peace or emerge from chronic social or economic conditions. The widespread use of irregular forces and terrorist tactics can be expected.[18]

---

[15]Ibid. Examples include the economic competition between the US and China and US assistance to the Congo to assist in training Congolese forces to combat insurgents.

[16]Ibid. Examples of stable peace include US involvement in Somalia, Bosnia, Kosovo, and Iraq when Operation New Dawn was executed during the summer of 2010.

[17]Ibid., 2-2.

[18]Ibid. This is not to say that a large number of military forces will not be used. Combined arms maneuver is understood to be when maneuver forces (for example, armor, infantry, and field artillery) perform their traditional roles in combat. The commitment of a large number of forces will most likely occur during an insurgency (the French had over five hundred thousand in Algeria), however many of those forces will be re-tasked from their original functions in order to best support the counterinsurgency campaign strategy. For example, the use of armor crewman to provide security by occupying border checkpoints and conducting dismounted patrols. Interstate and intrastate conflict includes the use of sanctuaries within other countries, such as Yemen during the Dhofar insurgency, and aid from adversarial governments, such as that provided by the Iranian Quds Force to Shia insurgents in southern Iraq.

General war is "armed conflict between major powers in which belligerents have used all their resources, and the national survival of a major belligerent is in jeopardy.[19] It occurs when diplomatic and economic channels are no longer functioning. Conflict will be characterized by the use of heavily armed conventional, guerilla, and unconventional forces that fight for military supremacy, and will end by exhaustion, defeat, or destruction of the military capabilities of one or more antagonists.[20]

Conflict is caused by a myriad of reasons, specific to the contexts of where they occur. For example, general warfare may occur when the peaceful political exchange between major powers regarding claims of ownership of rare resources fails. Conflict during general peace may be expressed through healthy economic competition. Conflict during periods of unstable peace and insurgency may originate from unresolved grievances between populations and the desire for increased political power.[21] Galula believed that insurgency was caused by the rise of nationalism and from communist

---

[19]Ibid. The national survival of a major belligerent may also be at risk during an insurgency.

[20]Ibid., 2-1. Author's analysis; the construct is not a perfect model, however, its utility to this chapter is that the construct acknowledges that conflict cannot be categorized into neat bins with limited interaction between each. The strength of the construct is the allowance of a conflict to transition along the scale into unstable peace or general war. Additionally, the author's experience has been to witness terms used incorrectly, which interferes with properly understanding a conflict's context. For example, 'stability operations', an element of full spectrum operations (i.e. offensive, defensive, and stability operations) is at times used as a synonym for peacekeeping operations, which is a joint military operation conducted within an operational theme.

[21]An example of conflict during unsteady peace is the Serb-Croat hostilities after NATO intervention in Kosovo; and the Chinese immigrants in Malaya are an example of conflict with the government. Exploitation of these grievances by an outside organization allows for the formation of an insurgency. For example, the Dhofari Liberation Front was co-opted by Yemeni communists at the beginning of the Dhofari insurgency in 1965.

pressure, and that there were three ways for a belligerent to take power: revolution, plot, and insurgency.[22]

Revolution, according to Galula, was the violent removal of the government by the populace. The masses mobilized in revolt, at the onset without a unified form of leadership; future leaders emerged as the revolution progressed. Plot was the overthrow of the government by a clandestine group. It did not involve the masses and required a long period of time and preparation. Insurgency had qualities similar to both plot and revolution. It was a protracted conflict requiring extensive planning and preparations executed methodically by an established leadership to achieve specific objectives, and required a degree of participation from the populace.[23]

Galula emphasized the importance of properly defining the conflict and identifying its adversaries so that the government could adapt to the situation, set objectives, and organize its forces to win.[24] The government had primacy over the military, and by having ultimate authority, was responsible for establishing the objectives of the conflict, not the military. The government's political, civil, and military agencies

---

[22]Galula, *Counterinsurgency Warfare, Theory and Practice*, 2, 96. This viewpoint can be expected from Galula. The French empire was in a state of decline during the 1950s as France lost influence in Indochina and Algeria while the Chinese and the Soviets were promoting communism in those regions.

[23]Ibid. Participation from the populace comes in the form of support (financial, material, sustenance), providing a source of new recruits, and possibly as victims.

[24]Galula, *Pacification in Algiers*, 244. He gave the example of a government believing they were combating criminals whereas their adversaries were an insurgent group conducting a war for independence. This was similar to the situation at the beginning of the Malayan Emergency, when the Malayan government had a business as usual attitude and considered the Chinese insurgents a criminal element. General Templer corrected their attitudes with the formation of the State War Executive Committee.

were responsible for creating and executing the strategies to achieve those objectives in an integrated, synchronized and coordinated manner at all levels of governance.[25]

Galula directly addressed the adaptation of both civilian and military organizations. He believed that the political, civil, and military organizations needed to be unified and their operations synchronized or they would fail. Because their operations overlapped, tasks and responsibilities could not be divided evenly amongst the three. The adaptation of the mindsets of the political and military leadership as well as those of the civilian population was also important, primarily to protect the legitimacy of the government and to secure popular support.[26]

The legitimacy of the government is at risk during periods of conflict. Kitson and Thompson both emphasized that the legitimacy of the government had to be preserved, which meant that all actions conducted by the government had to be done legally.[27] Laws must be enforceable and allow government actions, but may be modified or changed in

---

[25]Thompson, 50-52; Robert Komer, *The Malayan Emergency in Retrospect: Organization of a Successful Counterinsurgency Effort* (Santa Monica, CA: RAND, 1972), http://www.rand.org/pubs/reports/R957 (accessed 5 August 2011), 25-68; McCuen, *The Art of Counter-Revolutionary War*, 69; Kitson, 284. Thompson emphasized political primacy and stated that it was imperative that the government had a political endstate so that it did not become reactionary and enact ad hoc measures that undermined its legitimacy. Kitson, McCuen and Galula supported this principle, and stated that efforts should be unified, coordinated, and executed by the political, civil, and military agencies at all levels of the conflict. Kitson termed this 'good coordinating machinery.' The Malayan Emergency provides an example of an effective government organization integrated within the State and District Emergency War Councils (SWECs and DWECs). The SWECs and DWECs grouped government organizations under one chain of command in order to speed decision-making and place responsibility for counter-insurgency decisions with the civilian leadership.

[26]Galula, *Counterinsurgency Warfare, Theory and Practice*, 66.

[27]Kitson, 289.

order to prevent adversarial forces from exploiting loopholes. If laws were modified, it was the responsibility of the government to explain why changes were made to the populace. A public information campaign was required and a propaganda apparatus available to inform audiences of what changes were made and why, and to emphasize the lawfulness of the government's actions. The laws could be changed back once the conflict had been resolved.[28]

Galula added to the discussion on legitimacy by stating that rules of engagement were needed to protect both the government and soldiers. Soldiers would be protected legally, provided they followed the rules of engagement, and the government's legitimacy would be protected by preventing government forces from committing delegitimizing actions such as the accidental killing of civilians, illegal arrests or detainments or destroying private property. He believed that the political leadership needed to shift towards a more directive mindset and be willing to do what was necessary in order to win.[29]

The analytical construct of adaptability applied to a military organization requires that the military determine lines of effort that best support the government's political objectives, identify mission requirements, and appropriately task organize both its staffs

---

[28]Thompson, 52-55.

[29]Galula, *Counterinsurgency Warfare, Theory and Practice*, 67. An example is the use of population control, such as the use of village relocation by the British during the Malayan Emergency. Insurgent forces were receiving aid from villages. In order to stop the aid, one of the measures used was physically relocating the villages to locations that were not favorable to the insurgent forces. The decision to move the villages was a political decision, not military. Although an unpleasant decision to make, if was deemed necessary, and the Malayan government had to be willing to both issue the order and support the action as it was executed.

and maneuver units. A military organization is normally organized to fight within the context of general war.[30] Unstable peace and insurgency conflicts require specialized military units to address specialized tasks within the strategy.[31] Maneuver forces not structured to perform security operations would be re-tasked to best support the lines of effort.

Galula addressed this point when he commented on the immense scale of operations that would be required. The resources of the military were needed and soldiers, in the same manner as the political leadership, would be required to perform tasks outside of normal military operations.[32] An example is the previously mentioned use of an armor unit being tasked to conduct dismounted patrols and manning checkpoints.[33] The task organization of the staff sections was also important.

---

[30]This is referencing maneuver forces, such as armor, cavalry, and infantry, which normally have the majority of manpower within the US Army, instead of specialist units such as a Public Affairs Detachment.

[31]An example would be a civil affairs detachment executing civil capacity projects. Civil capacity operations normally restore, improve, and develop the delivery of essential services such as electricity, water, and sewage.

[32]Galula, *Counterinsurgency Warfare, Theory and Practice*, 61. He believed that the civil administrations were never up to the task of counter-insurgency. An example of this is the use of soldiers as schoolteachers during the Philippine insurgency of 1900. The author's experiences have been witnessing the re-tasking of specialty occupations, such as mechanics, cooks and administrative personnel, when like functions were provided by contractor services. Cooks and mechanics have been used as turret gunners and as personal security detachment members. Even though the resources of the military were required, the political leadership remained in control and established the objectives, not the military. Surrender of control from the political leadership to the military, in his opinion, was a sign of defeat.

[33]The author's experience while assigned to an armor battalion in Kosovo was being supported by an air defense battery tasked with conducting dismounted patrols and manning security checkpoints. Additionally, their Avenger weapons systems, which have

Military staffs are organized to perform a set range of duties and functions during general war.[34] Mission objectives and requirements may require specialized staff functions that are not inherent to a military organization's structure. For example, an armor battalion does not have a public affairs officer, a specialized staff position that appears on the table of organization at the brigade level and higher. If mission objectives required a public affairs officer, a member of the battalion would be tasked to perform those duties in addition to their normal responsibilities.[35]

The first analytical construct addressed the need for adaptability when organizing for, planning, and executing a campaign strategy during a period of conflict. Government forces must identify the type of conflict in which they are engaged. They must understand their adversary, and adapt politically, economically and militarily to win the conflict. Adaptation occurs both physically and mentally, and may require the re-tasking of government forces to execute the campaign strategy. The government must demonstrate the mental resolve required to win the conflict, which includes being directive and issuing the necessary orders to achieve the campaign objectives. The theorists suggested the use of a propaganda apparatus to execute the government's public information campaign.

---

an integrated video camera, thermal sight and .50 caliber machine gun, were used to observe smuggling routes.

[34]Department of the Army, FM 3-0, Appendix B. Normal US Army staff functions follow along the lines of administration, intelligence, operations, and sustainment. Additional and more specialized staff functions are available at higher levels of command.

[35]Author's example, based upon prior experience, provided to illustrate how a military organization can re-structure itself to meet mission requirements. Another example is the staff organization of the 1st Infantry Division in Iraq, one point of discussion within the Iraq case study.

This reference provides the linkage to the second analytical construct of understanding the relationship between security and civil capacity operations, and the information environment.[36]

Analytical construct two: Security, civil capacity, and the information environment

The host nation government has two means available to garner support from its population during periods of unstable peace and insurgency: the delivery of essential services and the provision of security from adversaries conducting violent actions against the population.[37] The delivery of essential services, such as electricity, water, and sewage, demonstrates the government's concern for the populace while addressing basic human needs. Providing education, medical care, and increased prosperity through economic opportunities demonstrates a government's commitment to improving the lives of its citizens. The provision of these services is ineffective if security within the environment does not exist.[38]

---

[36]Author's analysis.

[37]Author's analysis. This does not imply that security and civil capacity are the only means to securing public support. During periods of unstable peace and insurgency, they do become the most basic concerns for a populace and the potential source of grievances. During general war, defense of the populace from foreign invaders rises in importance.

[38]Thompson, 55; Kitson, 284; Galula, *Counterinsurgency Warfare, Theory and Practice*, 61; McCuen, *The Art of Counter-Revolutionary War,* 50; author's analysis. The provision of both security and essential services are not restricted to the government. Adversarial groups can and will provide the same. The challenge for the government is providing security and essential services to increase their legitimacy while delegitimizing adversarial organizations.

An adversary has the advantage at the beginning of a conflict. They are positioned to choose when and how to act and have the benefit of time to prepare propaganda in order to exploit their actions and discredit the government.[39] Thompson expanded on this perspective when he explained that whether adversaries were operating from safe havens located in remote places or from within urban areas, they would have influence over the population. It is defeating this influence that Thompson addressed when he said, "the government must give priority to defeating the political subversion, not the guerillas." Defeating the influence was the goal.[40]

Adversarial influence may be applied through coercion, enabled by familial ties, or facilitated by a shadow government that provided funding and resources to local insurgent cells.[41] The role of influence within periods of unstable peace and insurgency illustrated the connection between psychological action and security. McCuen addressed this connection when he stated that psychological action had an important role in the

---

[39]Kitson, 286.

[40]Thompson, 55-57. The French experience in Algieria and the Rhodesian military's experience during their insurgency is evidence that a counterinsurgency can be won militarily but lost politically. The French had effectively destroyed the Algerian insurgents, yet lost when the French government decided to grant independence to the Algerian National Liberation Front. The Rhodesians had a similar fate, having effectively rendered the insurgent organizations ineffective militarily, but failed to establish a narrative that resonated with the black communities. The result was the voting into political leadership by the Rhodesian populace of the very insurgent leadership they had been fighting against.

[41]Ibid.

mobilization of the masses and identified the target audience as the neutral members of the populace.[42]

McCuen stated that mobilizing the masses required more than winning the people over, that the insurgents' influence over the populace had to be neutralized or destroyed. This could be accomplished through force and the use of sanctions such as curfews, movement control, and relocation. The populace needed security in order to prevent adversarial reprisals and aid in presenting the government as a preferred alternative to supporting their adversaries.[43] Galula framed the importance of providing security in the form of two questions: which side was perceived as going to win; and which side threatened the most and/or offered the most protection?[44] Neutralizing adversarial influence is the defining element within the relationship between security and civil capacity.[45]

Civil capacity operations are the means for a host nation government to demonstrate commitment to providing for its populace, but without security, adversarial influence will neutralize government gains in the civil capacity arena. The population

---

[42]McCuen, *The Art of Counter-Revolutionary War*, 54. There are three broad groups of participants during unstable peace and insurgency: the adversaries and their supporters, the host nation government and its supporters, and the neutral members of the population. The neutral members of the population form the largest percentage of the participants.

[43]Ibid., 54.

[44]Galula, *Pacification in Algiers*, 246. Or more succinctly asked: who can hurt me now, and who will be here to hurt me later?

[45]Author's analysis. Security is required to neutralize influence on the population and enable civil capacity projects. Civil capacity projects neutralize adversarial influence and enables popular support to the government. Also, the focus on neutralizing influence establishes the connection between this thesis's second and third analytical constructs.

needs to be secured from adversaries, but that in and of itself is not enough. The neutral audiences need to be made aware of government successes in both security and civil capacity operations while simultaneously delegitimizing the adversarial narrative. Thompson, McCuen and Galula each expanded upon this point by linking the perception of government success to recommendations of how to conduct security operations.[46]

McCuen echoed Kitson when he said an adversary has the advantage of time and sanctuary, which allowed him to choose the place and time of his attacks. Government forces, on the other hand, were tasked with securing the nation, and in executing that task, were at risk of over-extending their resources. He suggested that the government, faced with exhausting itself, should set as its immediate objective the preservation of bases, populations, and forces. McCuen acknowledged the dilemma of whether to disperse to preserve critical areas or to concentrate in order to destroy the insurgents. He recommended security first. Once security had been established, the hunting of the insurgents could shift to the forefront of the government's efforts, and propaganda used to inform the populace of government success.[47] Through this approach, McCuen linked establishing security to mobilizing the masses and neutralizing adversarial influence.[48]

Thompson also recommended that the government establish secure base areas initially. Once the base areas had been secured, the government forces should

---

[46]Author's analysis.

[47]McCuen, *The Art of Counter-Revolutionary War*, 50-52.

[48]McCuen, *The Art of Counter-Revolutionary War*, 52; Thompson, 58; Galula, *Counterinsurgency Warfare, Theory and Practice*, 69. Thompson and Galula both supported reinforced McCuen's position when they emphasized the importance of the perception of security and government successes by the population.

methodically work outwards, gradually denying adversaries safe havens to operate from or within. Depending on the situation within the country, Thompson recommended securing an easily pacified area first; quick, initial successes would help inspire confidence in the people.[49] Galula recommended a similar approach.

Galula provided two broad approaches to selecting an area of operations: difficult-to-easy and easy-to-difficult. The difficult-to-easy approach concentrated on areas controlled by insurgent forces with expansion into less influenced areas as operations progressed. It was the quickest approach, provided it worked, because it destroyed the majority of the insurgent forces early on. The easy-to-difficult approach targeted areas under adversarial influence but not fully under their control. This approach required fewer resources, but was slower and gave the adversaries an opportunity to establish themselves in areas where they would be able to more easily exert their influence. Galula agreed with Thompson that it was better to operate from easy-to-difficult areas in order to demonstrate success to the population.[50] Kitson, Thompson, McCuen, and Galula, through their emphasis on the amplifying perceptions of success, emphasized the importance of the psychological dimension.

Kitson addressed the role of the psychological dimensions while cautioning against excessive, heavy handed, and reactionary actions by the government when attempting to restore peace and stability. The legitimacy of the government would be negatively affected by those kinds of actions and actively undermined by an adversary through the use of adversarial propaganda over-emphasizing government excesses and

---

[49]Thompson, 57-58.

[50]Galula, *Counterinsurgency Warfare, Theory and Practice*, 69.

failures. The government needed a counter-propaganda mechanism, using all means of information conduits (such as television, radio, and newspaper) to help prevent this.[51]

Thompson recommended that the government position itself to control information, whether through public information distributed by a variety of media conduits, or by an established intelligence apparatus. He suggested that a propaganda section, through the control of information, would allow government forces to force adversaries to expose themselves, amplify uncertainty within and between adversarial groups through misinformation, and inform audiences of the success of government operations. Propaganda efforts would emphasize the legitimacy of the government while simultaneously illustrating the unlawfulness of adversarial organizations.[52]

McCuen, as previously discussed, emphasized the role of a psychological apparatus applied to the mobilizing of the masses.[53] He also explained adversarial use of propaganda to attack the legitimacy of the government at both the national and international levels, and that an adversary would use every political, economic, educational, and psychological means in addition to force to accomplish their goals.

---

[51]Kitson, 286. Kitson cautioned that a government using the media to counter propaganda was at risk of being perceived of censorship. The government cannot afford to be viewed as manipulating, withholding and lying to its citizens. The use of propaganda, if not truthful or verifiable as true, can undermine the legitimacy of the government. For example, Sultan Qaboos of Oman controlled all information within his country, but was able to maintain his legitimacy by insisting on equitable news reporting within the Omani news service. Reports of successful civil capacity projects, such as the sinking of a well, was advertised to the Dhofari people by leaflet drop and radio broadcasts, but verified by eyewitness accounts spread through word of mouth conduits. See the Dhofari case study.

[52]Thompson, 55-57.

[53]McCuen, *The Art of Counter-Revolutionary War*, 52; Thompson, 58; Galula, *Counterinsurgency Warfare, Theory and Practice*, 69.

McCuen stressed that the government needed to recognize the scale of the conflict it was involved in, and commit itself to using every asset available in order to win. This recommendation included the integrated use of psychological operations and an intelligence section. McCuen reinforced the links between policy, government action and psychological operations, and credited adversaries for being equally capable of the same.[54]

Galula strongly supported the use of propaganda and psychological operations. He included their use within his strategies presented in *Counterinsurgency Warfare: Theory and Practice*, and suggested the integration of propaganda into government operations and against adversaries. He suggested using propaganda to minimize the affects of population control and arrests upon the populace, to advertise the importance of elections, exploit cooperation by the population, and prod adversarial forces into combat.[55] Galula demonstrated his support of military psychological operations units when he said the "mimeograph machine may be more useful than a machine gun."[56]

The review thus far has described the complexity of the operating environment within a conflict. Kitson said violence should be in support of ideas, and that counter-

---

[54]McCuen, *The Art of Counter-Revolutionary War*, 69.

[55]Galula, *Counterinsurgency Warfare: Theory and Practice*, chapter 7. Galula provided tactic, techniques, and procedures for the application of PSYOP to counter-insurgency strategies and against insurgents.

[56]Galula, *Counterinsurgency Warfare, Theory and Practice*, 66. A mimeograph machine is an old copy machine; its implied use in this case was to produce leaflets and flyers.

insurgent warfare was a contest for the minds of the population.[57] This 'contest' helps

establish the context of the convergent nature of conflict.

<u>Analytical construct three: The convergent nature of conflict</u>

Joint Publication (JP) 3-13, *Information Operations*, introduced the concept of the

environments of conflict, identified as air, land, space, electromagnetic, and

information.[58] The information environment, while considered distinct from the others,

was regarded as residing within each. It was made up of three interrelated dimensions:

physical, informational, and cognitive. The joint concept could be applied to the

discussion of the nature of conflict by expressing the five environments as three domains

similar to those of the information dimension.[59]

Joint Publication 3-13 defined the physical dimension as where the command and

control systems and the infrastructures that enabled operations across the sea, air, land,

and space domains resided. This included the location of physical platforms and

---

[57]Kitson, 282; McCuen, *The Art of Counter-Revolutionary Warfare*, 54-64; Galula, *Counterinsurgency Warfare*, 75-77, 90-92; Thompson, 50-52. Each theorist has proposed a similar viewpoint through their principles. McCuen addressed this contest in his principle 'Mobilizing the Masses', when he stated that the principle was about more than just winning the people over and that psychological action played an important role. Galula suggested exploiting the cooperation of the population through propaganda, or, at a minimum, obtaining their neutrality. Thompson advised restoring government authority, law and order to regain popular support.

[58]Department of Defense, Joint Publication 3-13, *Information Operations* (Washington, DC: Government Printing Office, February 2006), iv-5.

[59]Ibid.

communications systems, and combat power. This is the domain where physical actions take place.[60]

The informational domain was defined as "where information was collected, processed, stored, disseminated, displayed, and protected." This is the domain where information is sent and received. It is people talking to each other, spreading information, rumors, and propaganda. It is also the flow of information, which can be disrupted, corrupted, and usurped by any actor, from any sphere of influence.[61]

The cognitive dimension is the minds of the decision maker and target audiences. It is the dimension in which people think, perceive, visualize, and decide; and may be influenced by a number of factors, to include public opinion, the media, public information, and rumors.[62] This is the most difficult domain for government forces to operate within, however, according to the military theorists who say that insurgent warfare is the battle for people's minds, it is also the most important to win.

Broadening the information dimensions to be the domains of conflict establishes the context of the convergent nature of conflict. Events are executed in the physical domain, news of the events travel through the information domain and are received by decision makers and target audiences. The information can be intercepted, manipulated and modified by any actor. Adversaries will attempt to exploit physical attacks in order to have an effect upon targeted audiences, to include the local populace and the international community. Once received, the information causes an action in the receiver, which in

---

[60]Ibid., I-1.

[61]Ibid., I-2.

[62]Ibid.

24

turn may or may not aid the government forces' efforts.[63] Both McCuen and Hoffman

have provided concepts that support this extrapolation of joint military doctrine.

McCuen, while participating in the hybrid warfare debate,[64] pointed out that

within conflicts, intervening forces had to conduct traditional military operations while

simultaneously securing and stabilizing the population.[65] He continued this concept by

stating that hybrid conflicts were full spectrum wars with both physical and cognitive

dimensions.[66] Both government and interventionist forces were simultaneously fighting

against an armed enemy and attempting to control and support the population. This was

being done while also securing support from the international community. The

asymmetric element of hybrid war was not necessarily a new weapon system, but instead

the simultaneous execution of the conflict in the physical, informational, and cognitive

domains. Asymmetric battlegrounds extended beyond the conflict zone and home front

populations to the international community.[67] The points of vulnerability that contribute

to the perception of instability and complicate the cognitive domain are damaged,

destroyed, or disrupted security establishments, government offices and operations,

---

[63] Author's analysis.

[64] The author is not attempting to participate in the 'hybrid warfare' debate by referencing McCuen's, or other theorists', writings. The author wishes to maintain the integrity of McCuen's concept while more broadly applying his principles to help describe the convergent nature of conflict. For more pertaining to the hybrid warfare debate, the author recommends beginning with the works of John Arquilla, Colin S. Gray, and William J. Nemeth.

[65] John J. McCuen, "Hybrid Wars," *Military Review* (March-April 2008): 108. This is an element of McCuen's definition of hybrid warfare.

[66] Ibid.

[67] Ibid., 107.

military sites and forces, essential services, and the economy. These areas, according to McCuen, were the battlegrounds of legitimacy and were where conflicts were lost.[68]

McCuen stated three strategic end states for hybrid warfare: to conduct conventional operations that targeted governmental, political, security and military structures with a consideration for the affects of the operations; clearing, controlling, and counter-organizing the population; and winning and maintaining support from both the nation's population and the international community.[69]

"Both the insurgent's conventional and information operations are designed to protract the war and gain outside support, thereby wearing down their enemies."[70] The adversarial strategy was to conduct protracted violence within the population, targeting and attacking the above-mentioned points of vulnerability and exploiting the effects of those attacks in the informational and cognitive domains. This is much like the nature of insurgent warfare discussed by Kitson, Thompson, Galula and Hoffman.

Lieutenant Colonel (Retired) Frank Hoffman, while also writing in regard to the hybrid warfare debate, expressed the concept as the evolving character of conflict, which he defined as convergence. This included the "convergence of the physical and psychological, the kinetic and nonkinetic, and combatants and noncombatants." Additionally, Hoffman included military force and the interagency community, states and

---

[68]Ibid., 108.

[69]Ibid., 111.

[70]Ibid.,109.

26

nonstate actors, and the capabilities they were armed with.[71] This was very similar to

McCuen's viewpoint that an adversary will use every asset at their disposal and all forms

of war to win.[72]

Similar to the spectrum of war presented by FM 3-0, Hoffman saw the dissolution

of distinct operational types. Without using the articulation of the three domains of

conflict, Hoffman described their interrelated nature when he said "multi-modal activities

can be conducted by separate units, or even by the same unit, but are generally

operationally and tactically directed and coordinated within the main battlespace to

achieve synergistic effects in the physical and psychological dimensions of conflict."[73]

Physical actions are conducted to have a psychological affect, or paraphrasing Kitson,

violence would be used in the support of ideas.

Chapter conclusions

The context of modern warfare has changed, but the nature of war itself has not.[74]

Although Kitson, Thompson, McCuen, and Galula's principles should be viewed within

the context of the conflicts in which they were developed, they do provide observations

that are applicable to modern conflict. The link between their principles and the

convergent nature of conflict is the understanding of the convergence of the domains in

---

[71]Frank G. Hoffman, "Hybrid Warfare and Challenges," *Joint Forces Quarterly* (1st Quarter 2009), 34.

[72]Ibid., 35.

[73]Ibid.

[74]Hoffman, *Joint Forces Quarterly,* 36. Or as Hoffman said, "Hybrid wars are not new, but they are different.

27

which conflict will occur: the physical, informational, and cognitive. Adversaries will pursue violence not only with physical attacks, but also through the manipulation and interference with information and the systems in which it is transmitted, and within the minds of populations and those who oppose them.

Hoffman recommended applying an innovative approach to thinking about modern conflict.[75] The extrapolation of the three domains of conflict from the joint doctrine, along with the other two analytical constructs, is an attempt by the author to do just that. The three analytical constructs will be used to conduct the case studies of the British during the Dhofar Insurgency, and the 1st Infantry Division in southern Iraq during Operation Iraqi Freedom and Operation New Dawn. A review of the doctrinal evolution of information operations is needed in order to fully understand the role that information operations has within the three analytical constructs.

---

[75]Hoffman, *Joint Forces Quarterly*, 38.

CHAPTER 3

THE DOCTRINAL EVOLUTION OF INFORMATION OPERATIONS

An understanding of the doctrinal evolution of information operations (IO) is required in order to establish the connection between IO and the convergent nature of the physical, informational, and cognitive domains of conflict. The IO concept was first introduced to the US Army in 1995 in the Training and Doctrine Command (TRADOC) Pamphlet 525-69,[76] and was defined as "the integrated approach to gaining and maintaining the information the warfighter requires to fight and win, while denying that same kind of information to adversaries."[77] Although this was the first occurrence of the term 'information operations', it was not the origin of the discipline. Information operations' origin is linked to 1978 when the Department of Defense developed the concept of command, control, and communications countermeasure warfare (C3CM) in direct response to the Soviet electronic warfare threat, called Radioelectronic Combat (REC), of the Cold War. The concept of information operations within the US Army and the Department of Defense has gradually evolved from a technical approach that targeted command and control systems to a broader concept that included the integrated application of non-technical capabilities such as psychological operations (PSYOP) and public affairs (PA).

---

[76]Department of the Army, TRADOC PAM 525-69, *Military Operations Concept for Information Operations,* August 1, 1995, http://iwar.org.uk/iwar/resources/tradoc/p525-69.htm (accessed August 2, 2011).

[77]Ibid., foreward.

The REC response

Soviet REC doctrine called for the total integration of electronic warfare, physical destruction, and deception resources to disrupt an enemy's use of their command and control systems, and focused on the use of technical assets to accomplish its goals.[78] Soviet REC was an integrated electronic warfare system that combined signals intelligence, direction finding, intensive jamming, deception, and destructive fires. Its purpose was to limit, delay, or nullify enemy C2 while protecting Soviet systems, with the goal of destroying or disrupting a majority of enemy's C2 and weapon system communications. This was accomplished through jamming, destructive fires, and deception. The Soviets understood that it was not possible to fully cripple an enemy's C2 network; therefore they sought to disrupt an enemy's 'critical time phasing' so that perishable information became obsolete.[79]

The Soviet military depended upon accurate and timely intelligence, provided by electronic intercept and direction finding measures to detect targets, to execute REC operations. Electronic intercept, also known as radio intercept, was the ability to monitor and understand message content, which provided target locations through normal

---

[78]Department of the Army, Field Manual (FM) 100-2-1, *The Soviet Army: Operations and Tactics* (Washington, DC: Government Printing Office, July 16, 1984), chapter 15. Field Manual 100-2-1, discusses REC in detail. US Army doctrinal development during the post-Vietnam period was a time of reconstruction for the US Army. General Dupuy formed the Training and Doctrine Command and instituted a re-writing of US Army doctrine as a ways to recover from the debilitating affects of the Vietnam War. The Soviet Union was identified as the threat for doctrine to be developed against, which may help explain why the early concepts of information operations had a technical focus.

[79]Ibid., 15-1. Critical time phasing is defined as the collection and reporting of data, evaluation and decision, issuance of orders and preparation, and completion of action.

command messages and situation reports. Transmitting stations were detected by their

electromagnetic emissions (i.e. radio transmissions), which were in turn used to develop

enemy situation templates and to target enemy indirect fire assets, radars and jammers.[80]

Command posts, observation posts, communications centers, and radar stations

ranked high on targeting priority lists and were eliminated by either physical destruction

or jamming. Indirect fire, ground attack (primarily by special operations forces) and air

attack means were used to execute physical destruction missions. Jamming was used

when physical destruction was not possible.[81]

Either physical actions or electronic deception were used to execute REC

deception operations. Physical actions were the use of dummies and decoys to simulate

activity where there was none. Electronic deception used antiradar jamming camouflage

and provided false information on troops, movements, and equipment over

communications networks.[82]

The US military's response, command, control, and communications

countermeasure warfare (C3CM) was an almost duplicate of REC. The C3CM concept,

introduced in 1978 in Department of Defense Directive 4600.4, was electronic warfare

centric, and was defined as: "the integrated the use of operations security, military

deception, jamming, and physical destruction, supported by intelligence, to deny

---

[80]Ibid.

[81]Ibid., 15-1 to 15-6.

[82]Lieutenant Colonel D. B. Lawrence, "Sovietelectronic Combat," *Air Force Journal* (March 1982), http://www.airforce-magazine.com/MagazineArchive/Pages/ 1982/March%201982/0382radioelectronic.aspx (accessed July 31, 2011). Deception was used as a protective measure.

information to influence, degrade, or destroy adversary command, control, and

communications capabilities and to protect friendly C3 against such actions."[83]

Electronic warfare (EW),[84] through deceptive radio transmissions and jamming, was the

implied primary means to disrupt adversarial commander C2 systems. The inclusion of

military deception (MILDEC),[85] operations security (OPSEC),[86] jamming (electronic

warfare) and physical destruction (PD)[87] was an attempt to combine different military

disciplines similar to those used by REC, with the aims of severing an enemy

---

[83]Department of Defense. Department of Defense Directive 3222.4, *Electronic Warfare (EW) and Command, Control, and Communications Countermeasures (C3CM)* (Washington, DC: Government Printing Office, July 31, 1992).

[84]Department of the Army, Field Manual (FM) 3-13, *Information Operations*, (Washington, DC: Government Printing Office, November 2003), 2-7. Electronic warfare is defined as any military action involving the use of electromagnetic and directed energy to control the electromagnetic spectrum or to attack the enemy.

[85]Ibid., 2-6. FM 3-13 defines military deception as actions executed to deliberately mislead adversary military decision makers as to friendly military capabilities, intentions, and operations, thereby causing the adversary to take specific actions (or inactions) that will contribute to the accomplishment of the friendly mission.

[86]Ibid., 2-2. FM 3-13 defines Operations security as a process of identifying essential elements of friendly information and subsequently analyzing friendly actions attendant to military operations and other activities to: identify those actions that can be observed by adversary intelligence systems, determine indicators hostile intelligence systems might obtain that could be interpreted or pieced together to deceive essential elements of friendly information time to be useful to adversaries, and to select and execute measures that eliminate or reduce to an acceptable level the vulnerabilities of friendly actions to adversary exploitation.

[87]Ibid., 2-11. FM 3-13 defines physical destruction in US Army doctrine as the application of combat power to destroy or degrade adversary forces, sources of information, command and control systems, and installations. It includes direct and indirect fires from ground, sea, and air forces. Also included are direct fire actions by special operations forces.

commander's communications links, under a single controlling concept.[88] Influencing

was expressed in the context of jamming, electronic deception, and/or physical coercion,

not through the context of information engagement, as it would be by the US Army in the

early part of the twenty-first century.[89] The next doctrinal change of C3CM was

influenced by an increased focus on the rise in the value of information, especially

information being manipulated in the media and by actors not directly involved in

military operations.[90]

The role of information

The use of the media by both the US military and adversaries was not a new

occurrence. For example, insurgents during the Philippine Insurgency, 1899 to1901,

attempted to influence the US presidential elections in favor of William Jennings Bryant.

Their intent was to influence American popular opinion through a protracted conflict and

by using propaganda emphasizing US military atrocities against native Filipinos. The

Filipino insurgents viewed Bryant, a firm opponent to the Filipino War as the presidential

candidate sympathetic to their cause, and believed that once elected, he would likely

---

[88]Tara Leweling and Ron Walters, "The Evolution of US Military Conceptions of Information Warfare and Information Operations, 1979-2004: An Initial Report," in *4th European Conference on Information Warfare and Security*, ed. Bill Hutchinson (Academic Conferences Limited, July 2005), 198.

[89]Ibid.

[90]That is not to say that the media, or any other actor for that matter, previously in history had not manipulated information, only that the military was placing greater emphasis on the fact.

remove the US military forces from the Philippines and grant independence.[91] What differentiates the media and information apart from the Philippine Insurgency and other previous periods is the speed at which information could be transmitted and the ease of its manipulation by a wider audience.

Field Manual 100-6, *Information Operations*, 1996, introduced the concept of the global information environment (GIE) paradigm.[92] The GIE was defined as an expanding information domain that included "all individuals, organizations, or systems, most of which are outside the control of military or National Command Authorities, that collect, process, and disseminate information to national and international audiences."[93] Within the GIE was the military information environment (MIE), defined as "the environment contained within the GIE, consisting of information systems and organizations, friendly and adversary, military and non-military, that support, enable or significantly influence a specific military operations." The MIE addressed the affect of information at the

---

[91]Anthony James Joes, "Counterinsurgency in the Philippines 1898-1954," in *Counterinsurgency in Modern Warfare*, eds. Daniel Marston and Carter Malkasian (Oxford: Osprey Publishing, 2010), 46. Brian Linn, *The Philippine War, 1899-1902* (Lawrence, KS: University of Kansas Press, 2000) is another excellent reference.

[92]Department of the Army, Field Manual (FM) 100-6, *Information Operations,* (Washington, DC: Government Printing Office, 1996), 1-2; Department of the Army, Field Manual (FM) 46-1*, Public Affairs* (Washington, DC: Government Printing Office, May 1997), 10. The manipulation of information in the GIE was the perceived threat. The information environment descriptions are presented out of doctrinal development order to serve the purpose of explaining the doctrinal influences upon information operations as the concept matured during the 1990s. MOP 30 was released prior to FM 100-6; the author makes the assumption that the information environment discussion was being shared by the writers of both documents, and thus influenced the writing of both.

[93]Ibid.

operational and tactical levels of war, whereas the GIE addressed the affect of information at all levels of war and outside periods of crisis and conflict.

Doctrine writers recognized that the effects of global communications and the media were to accelerate and expand the collective awareness of populations. Information could be used to "ignite passions, spark new perspectives, compel people, and crystallize deeply held beliefs"[94] and coupled with the rapid development of information technology, influence the changing context of warfare.[95]

Military practitioners viewed the GIE a source of information with the capability of having an affect on military operations. Adversaries were in a position to cause a

---

[94]FM 100-6, *Information Operations*, 1-1. As stated earlier, the military was now placing an emphasis on a phenomenon that had been occurring repeatedly throughout history. The control of information to the media was a tactic used by the Dhofari Information Section during the Dhofar insurgency. Filipino insurgents attempted to use the media to influence US presidential elections. The media heavily affected popular support to the Vietnam War. The leadership of the United States applied propaganda to the US populace during World War Two, evidenced for example by OPSEC posters, war bond advertisements, and Hollywood movies such as *Bataan*. What sets this period apart from others is the doctrinal movement to gather resources and capabilities that were able to exploit the role of information in the MIE together under a single doctrinal umbrella.

[95]TRADOC Pam 525-69, foreword. This is a relative statement based upon an observer's concept of 'fast'. In 1900, fast was the sending and receiving of a message within twenty-four hours. In 2011, the transmission and receipt of a message is measured within milli-seconds. Also, the US Army continued to invest in computerization and information technology. The author's experiences with information technology began in 1987 with the use of the digital message device, a small but bulky dedicated computer used to digitally transmit calls for artillery fires. Computers used for administrative tasks were a rarity in 1995 and were the property of staff officers. In 2000, there was one computer, used to write evaluation reports and award submissions, available to the platoon leaders of the author's maneuver company. By 2004, nearly every US Army leader and administrative personnel would have a computer workstation and nearly all members of the military linked by e-mail. This 'connectedness' is what the writers of the GIE and MIE were describing. Additionally, this statement does not imply that the context of war had been stagnant until the 1990s, merely that military was placing a greater focus on the manipulation of information during military operations.

reaction with little to no effort or risk; and information could be used to compress the public's perception of the levels of war, allowing a quick bridging between tactical operations and national military goals.[96] Doctrine writers acknowledged that this would be a challenge to commanders, and that the GIE should be considered in all future military operations.[97]

The affect of the GIE paradigm was that the US Army became convinced that C3CM needed to transition from a 'concept' to something more relevant to warfighting. The result was the information warfare and information operations concepts. Three documents, Memorandum of Policy 30, TRADOC Pam 525-69, and FM 100-6, *Information Operations* guided the development of and implementation of these concepts.

The IO construct

Memorandum of Policy (MOP) Number 30, version 1, dated 8 March 1993 changed C3CM to Command and Control Warfare (C2W). Policy makers included psychological operations (PSYOP) along with MILDEC, OPSEC, EW, and PD as the core capabilities and five principal military actions integrated under C2W.[98] The C2W

---

[96]Ibid., 2-1.e.1. It is during this period that PSYOP began to merge with the C2W concept.

[97]This echoes the political aspects of counterinsurgent warfare and the use of propaganda to fight for the minds of the population. Kitson, Thompson, McCuen, and especially Galula all emphasized this aspect within their principles. The compression of the levels of war is a descriptor of the convergent nature of conflict.

[98]Chairman of the Joint Chiefs of Staff, "Memorandum of Policy 30, version 1," *Command and Control Warfare* (Washington, DC: Government Printing Office, March 8, 1993). The inclusion of PSYOP as a core capability was possibly due to the affect PSYOP had on Iraqi soldiers during Desert Storm. Doctrine writers recognized the role of

definition was similar to that of C3CM, using the term 'electronic warfare' instead of 'jamming' and the C2W tasks differed solely by the change in verbiage from C3CM to C2. The strengths of the revision were the refocusing of C2W on warfighting, and the narrowing of C2W's focus to the five 'pillars'.[99]

The memorandum emphasized the importance of timely information flow to the warfighter and linked how information was related to command and control functions such as personnel, equipment, communications, computers, facilities, and procedures. These systems were vulnerable to adversarial actions, such as MILDEC, PSYOP, EW, and PD, which had the potential to degrade one or more of the components, causing doubt and limiting the effectiveness of the command and leadership structure.[100]

There were three other significant differences between MOP 30 and DODD 4600.4. The directives ordered commanders to designate a single staff component to be responsible for C2W integration into operations; commanders were given the authority to re-organize their staffs as they deemed necessary; and, the directives placed emphasis on C2W's integrative nature by stating, "all warfighting capabilities potentially may be

---

PSYOP in influencing Iraqi soldiers to surrender. Although difficult to prove that PSYOP leaflets were directly responsible for the surrenders, the leaflets at least provided instructions on how to do so. This is a similar observation to the Dhofar Information Section's use of leaflet drops to encourage *adoo* surrenders in Oman during the 1970s. Additionally, MOP 30 is a joint document, written to be general in nature to allow each service component to implement its guidance in accordance with their respective missions and capabilities.

[99]Ibid., 3.

[100]Ibid.

employed" with the "level of applicability of each being conditioned by the circumstances and resources available."[101]

TRADOC Pam 525-69, released in 1 August 1995, provided additional refinement to the C2W definition and introduced both information operations (IO) and information warfare (IW) to US Army doctrine. The doctrine writers of TRADOC Pam 525-69 defined information operations as the broader construct of the five core capabilities "executed across the full range of operations-peace, operations other than war, lesser regional contingencies/major regional contingencies, and war integrated within joint, multinational, and/or interagency operations and throughout all phases of force-projection operations and at all levels of war."[102] According to the new reference, IO was IW conducted throughout the full spectrum of conflict, whereas IW was IO conducted during crisis or conflict. This distinction between IO and IW was made as an attempt to work within the interagency process. Non-military governmental agencies chose to use 'information operations' because the phrase was viewed as less threatening at the strategic level.[103] Information operations became the phrase used to reference

---

[101]Ibid., 6. The issue with this guidance is that it is too general; the core capabilities were not true capabilities, instead a collection of assets and operations. Military deception and PD are not capabilities or assets; they are operations. Electronic warfare has clearly tasked assets with which to conduct operations; therefore it is a capability. Finally, the effectiveness of C2W would rest upon the personal initiative of the staff officer assigned to plan and implement C2W into operations and the level of comfort a commander had in its use.

[102]TRADOC Pam 525-69, 3-1.i. This is an US Army definition.

[103]Leweling and Walters, 199.

38

interagency operations and IW used to denote military operations. Command and control warfare was the "military strategy that implement[ed] information warfare."[104]

Field Manual 100-6, *Information Operations*, published 27 August 1996, further refined the implementation of the IO construct and added CA and PA as capabilities under the IO umbrella. The manual's writers acknowledged that the "traditional focus when discussing information and C2 was electronic warfare, electronic countermeasure, and electronic counter countermeasure operations that [took] place during war,"[105] yet made the linkage between C2W and the GIE, and the affect of both the media and global information systems on military operations. Information operations were information warfare conducted through all phases of conflict and all levels of war. Information warfare was IO conducted during crisis or conflict, and was comprised of C2W (MILDEC, EW, PD, PSYOP, and OPSEC), civil affairs (CA), and public affairs (PA).[106]

Refinement of the IO concept within the US Army would come in 2003 with the release of FM 3-13, *Information Operations*.[107] The manual categorized threat

---

[104]TRADOC Pam 525-69, 1-5.c; was citing DoDD TS-3600.1, which is not available due to security classifications.

[105]FM 100-6, preface.

[106]Ibid. The inclusion of civil affairs and public affairs as elements of IO, grouped with the technical capabilities of C2W, creates the impression that the doctrine writers were struggling with a changing environment that was beginning to outstrip their ingrained tradition of thought. The author presents the observation that the doctrine writers did not want to separate EW from a construct on which they had worked hard to establish. Electronic warfare does not have much in common with PA and CA. The logical step at this time would have been to divest IO of the EW mission. Emerging doctrine, discussed in greater detail at the conclusion of this chapter, attempts to correct this issue.

[107]Department of Defense. *Information Operations Roadmap* (Wahington, DC: Department of Defense, 2003). Donald Rumsfeld, the Secretary of Defense in 2003,

capabilities, sources and methods, which implied that the targeting approach of C2W remained within the doctrine. The methods of attack were mostly through technical applications (primarily electronic warfare based), and introduced perception management. The GIE was shortened to information environment and was "defined as the aggregate of individuals, organizations, or systems that collect, process, or disseminate information."[108]

Field Manual 3-13 maintained a similar purpose of IO to that of C2W, the "attacking [of] adversary command and control (C2) systems (offensive IO) while protecting friendly C2 systems from adversary disruption (defensive IO)" with the purpose of establishing information superiority.[109] Emphasis was placed on achieving information domination with a focus on the use of technology through the use of computer network operations (CNO) and EW. Field Manual 3-13 grouped the capabilities into three categories (core capabilities, supporting capabilities, and related capabilities) and placed them under a special staff officer, the assistant chief of staff G7.[110] The

---

oversaw the conduct of this study. The findings were reported in the *Information Operations Roadmap*, and the recommendations of the report were included in FM 3-13, *Information Operations*. The report concluded that effectively communicating the US governments capabilities and intentions and the ability to rapidly disseminate persuasive information were a key assumption of the importance of IO. Although the report continued to address the importance of the use of the traditional core capabilities, emphasis would gradually be placed on influencing audiences through soft power applications. This helped to create a media-only focus for IO, which contributes to the current debate of what IOs purpose is.

[108]Department of the Army, Field Manual (FM) 3-13, *Information Operations* (Washington, DC: Government Printing Office, 2003), 1-2.

[109]Ibid., v.

[110]Ibid., 1-1. This was a refinement to the guidance given in MOP 30.

definition of IO was re-written as "the employment of the core capabilities of electronic warfare, computer network operations, psychological operations, military deception, and operations security, in concert with specified supporting and related capabilities, to affect or defend information and information systems, and to influence decision-making."[111]

The core capabilities became EW, CNO (including network attack, defense, and exploitation), PSYOP, OPSEC, and MILDEC. Physical destruction was removed as a core capability and grouped as a supporting capability along with information assistance, physical security, counter intelligence, counter deception, counter propaganda public affairs, civil military operations, and "any activity that contributes to gaining and maintaining information superiority" became related capabilities.[112]

Field Manual 3-13 defined perception management as "actions to convey and/or deny selected information and indicators to foreign audiences to influence their emotions, motives, and objective reasoning."[113] Perception management collected the non-technical capabilities normally tasked with executing public affairs operations, OPSEC, deception, and PSYOP under its umbrella concept. Department of Defense Directive 3600.01 released August 2006 would provide additional refinement.

---

[111]Ibid., 1-13.

[112]Ibid. Field Manual 3-13, 2003, expanded upon the concepts of FM 100-6 by adding supporting and related capabilities. The doctrine writers refined the information environment construct, stratified the threats operating within the environment, and applied a systematic approach to the integration of IO into operations. The strength of the manual was that it attempted to provide techniques for the execution of IO. The weakness was that it implied that the G-7 was the subject matter expert for all of the capabilities. Additionally, the inclusion of any other activity that contributes to maintaining information superiority is similar to the guidance from MOP 30.

[113]Ibid., 1-7.

The DoDD 3600.01 definition of IO maintained the core, supporting, and related capabilities and better articulated the tasks to be "influence, disrupt, corrupt, or usurp adversarial human and automated decision making while protecting our own."[114] The DoDD 3600.01 also provided guidance on how IO would be applied during periods of crisis, conflict, and post conflict and stability operations. During periods of crisis, IO would be used as a flexible deterrent option used to communicate the US governments intentions and resolve; and during conflict, IO would achieve both physical and psychological results in support of combat operations. In post conflict and stability operations, IO would continue to influence foreign perceptions.[115] Field Manual 3-0, *Operations* (2008), reworked perception management into information engagement (IE) and reduced the G7's tasks to inform and influence.

The information engagement period

Field Manual 3-0, *Operations*, released February 2008, restructured IO. The emphasis on information superiority was kept, however IO became refocused on "peoples' perceptions, beliefs, and behavior to the success or failure of full spectrum operations and in the persistent conflicts the nation continues to face."[116] The five core

---

[114]Department of Defense, Department of Defense Directive O-3600.1, *Information Operations* (Washington, DC: Government Printing Office, August 14, 2006), 1.

[115]Ibid., 2. This clarification of ways of implementing IO into operations should have been helpful to the US Army. The author does not believe that to be the case because of the debates regarding the purposes and functions of IO as evidenced by available writings. It is the author's opinion that the guidance was not widely known nor disseminated.

[116]Department of the Army, Field Manual (FM) 3-0, *Operations* (Washington, DC: Government Printing Office, 2008), 7-2. Information Operations was not a clearly

capabilities were divided into information tasks (IE, command and control warfare, information protection, OPSEC, and MILDEC), which were then distributed across the staff. The G7 became responsible for IE, defined as "the integrated employment of public affairs to inform U.S. and friendly audiences; psychological operations, combat camera, U.S. Government strategic communication and defense support to public diplomacy, and other means necessary to influence foreign audiences; and, leader and Soldier engagements to support both efforts."[117] The G7's responsibilities were reduced to integrating soldier and key leader engagements, public affairs, PSYOP, combat camera, and defense support to public diplomacy. Legitimacy, for both the US and host nation governments became the center of gravity, and IE was seen as the means to help achieve it.[118]

---

understood concept, even thirteen years after it inception. The shift from IO to IE, and the media focus that accompanied the shift confused Io to both PA and PSYOP, increased confusion, and spurred many debates as to what IO was. Searching the Command and General Staff College library will provide numerous theses and monographs providing (Department of Defense 2011)opposing viewpoints and insights on IO, as well as debates as to what is the purpose of IO.

[117]Ibid., 7-3. Information operations had evolved to be more soft power focused than before. The author proposes that a possible source of the confusion surrounding IO is not that it is a soft power discipline, but more because the results of IO are difficult to measure. Operations and capabilities such as EW, MILDEC, and OPSEC are easier to measure because there are normally physical indicators. If an enemy radio ceases to transmit after being jammed by an EW attack, then the attack can be deemed a success. The results of PSYOP and IE are difficult to measure because the effect occurs within the cognitive domain. For example, the reason for Iraqi soldiers surrendering during Operation Desert Storm are hard to determine. They may have surrendered because of the US PSYOP leaflets encouraging their surrender, or they may have surrendered because of the one hundred hours of tactical bombing they had endured.

[118]CB20110930H0002, interview by Darrell Vaughan, Fort Leavenworth, KS, September 30, 2011. A single individual from within the IO Proponent Office introduced this doctrinal change and did not formally staff the doctrine through both the US Army and the Department of Defense. There was large-scale resistance to IE, which limited

The IE concept, integrated with the redesigned information tasks, was introduced into the Functional Area 30, Information Operations (FA 30) qualification course taught at the Information Operations Proponent Office, Fort Leavenworth, Kansas. Information engagement was an emerging doctrinal construct and was taught in conjunction with the older doctrine of FM 3-13, 2003. Resistance to IE was strong both with FA30s and from the joint operations community, and was abandoned by 2010.[119]

<u>Emerging IO doctrine</u>

Information Operations' doctrine changed again in 2011. The Honorable Robert M. Gates, Secretary of Defense in January 2011, issued a DoD memorandum directing a change in the IO definition to "the integrated employment, during military operations, of information-related capabilities in concert with other lines of operation to influence, disrupt, corrupt, or usurp the decision-making of adversaries and potential adversaries

---

FA30s to the capacity of a public relations specialist, a responsibility of the public affairs office, or as a layman PSYOP officer. The IE focus was supported by the experiences of commanders and FA30s at the battalion and brigade levels of operations, which have limited resources with which to conduct IO. Operations at those levels are primarily media and PSYOP focused, and justified the viewpoint that IO was just a synonym for either media relations or PSYOP. The IE doctrine did not account for division level and higher capabilities and operations.

[119]CB20110930H0002, interview; CB20110831H0001, interview by Darrell Vaughan, Fort Leavenworth, KS, August 31, 2011; CB20110830W0001, interview by Darrell Vaughan, Fort Leavenworth, KS, August 30, 2011. The loss of ownership of the capabilities associated with IO under the IE construct became another point of confusion and debate within the US Army. The FA30 community maintained that they owned the capabilities. The counter argument was that it was unlikely that an FA30 was a subject matter expert over such a disparate collection of capabilities. The distinction between integrator and capability provider became blurred.

while protecting our own."[120] Focus was on the integrative nature of IO and deliberately

avoided placing emphasis on core capabilities. The reasoning was that the old definitions

had an excessive focus on capabilities and their ownership, which "confused the

distinction between them and IO as an integrating staff function."[121] Field Manual 3-0,

change 1, went an additional step by changing the name of IO to inform and influence

activities (IIA).[122] Inform and influence activities were defined as the "integrating

activities within the mission command warfighting function which ensures themes and

messages designed to inform domestic audiences and influence foreign friendly, neutral,

adversary, and enemy populations."[123]

Emerging doctrinal changes redefined the information environment, provided a

clarified and stratified classification of IO related military professionals, and

acknowledged that capabilities traditionally thought of as IO are only information related

capabilities when used to support IO. The currently unpublished revision to DoDD

3600.01 refined the definition of information environment by addressing the

---

[120]Robert M. Gates, Memorandum for Secretaries of the Military Departments, *Strategic Communication and Information Operations in the DoD* (Washington, DC: Government Printing Office, January 25, 2011), 2.

[121]Ibid.

[122]Department of the Army, FM 3-0, 6-15. For consistency, the term IO will be used for the remainder of this thesis.

[123]Ibid., 6-15. This change came about as both a result of the doctrinal lessons learned from US Army involvement Iraq and Afghanistan and the debate regarding the purpose and integration of IO into operations. Practitioners were too wed to the notion of owning capabilities, and commanders provided guidance to their IO staff officers based upon what their experiences had been. This also similar to the guidance provided in MOP 30.

manipulation of information by any actor.[124] The information environment was defined as "the aggregate of individuals, formal and informal organizations, and the systems they use, both individually and in networks, to generate, collect, process, manipulate, disseminate, manage, and employ information."[125]

The IO force was stratified into three categories: information-related capability specialists, IO planners, and intelligence personnel dedicated to supporting IO.[126] Information-related capability specialists included those trained professionals who, for example, conduct EW, CNO, and PSYOP.[127] Information operations planners were FA30s and any other individual serving in an IO planning and integration role. For example, a PSYOP officer serving in a PSYOP planner position within a division headquarters versus a PSYOP planner serving as a planner in a PSYOP battalion; the distinction is that the planner within the battalion is focused on PSYOP pure operations, whereas the planner on division staff is focused on the integration of PSYOP operations into a broader division plan. The inclusion of intelligence personnel as part of the IO

---

[124]Department of Defense, Department of Defense Directive 3600.01 (Washington, DC: Government Printing Office, 2011); CB20110831H0001, interview. The manipulation of information by any actor is a recurring theme in information operations doctrine. The author's opinion is that the inclusion of this observation in policy directives strengthens the development of IO doctrine.

[125]Ibid., 2; CB20110831H0001, interview.

[126]Ibid.

[127]This is not an all-inclusive listing of IO capabilities.

46

force was progressive on the part of the US Army doctrine developers. This category

included analysts dedicated to analyzing IO specific intelligence.[128]

Finally, the DoDD 3600.01 Draft identified information-related capabilities, again

not an all-inclusive list, as combat camera, CNO, PSYOP,[129] EW, MILDEC, and OPSEC

with the caveat of they are only information-related capabilities when used in support of

IO.[130] The inclusion of the caveat recognizes that the capabilities have other

responsibilities and applications and are not always functioning in support of IO. For

example, the use of protective EW to provide convoy defense against remote detonated

IEDs is an example of EW not used in support of IO.

The doctrine had come full circle returning IO (now IIA) to an integrating staff

function and broadened the discipline by not limiting IO to a specific set of capabilities

with inform and influence as its only tasks.[131] Emerging doctrine resembled the doctrine

of FM 3-13, 2003, but with a better understanding of the information environment and

how IO related capabilities integrated with one another. The FA30 was clearly identified

as a specialized staff planner with enough of a working knowledge of specialized

---

[128]Examples are the author's analysis. The inclusion of intelligence personnel is an empowering move by the IO community. Although it doesn't change the duties of an analyst, their being linked more closely to the IO community changes their focus when providing IO support.

[129]Gates; CB20110831H0001, interview; CB20110930H0002, interview. The name of PSYOP was officially changed to Military Information Support Operations (MISO) along with the change of IO to Inform and Influence activities in January 2011. The acronym PSYOP will be used throughout this thesis in order to avoid confusion.

[130]Ibid.

[131]FM 3-13, *Information Operations, Draft*, (Unpublished), 1-3. This version of FM 3-13 is currently being written and staffed within the Department of Defense. The tasks of IO include destroy, disrupt, degrade, deny, deceive, exploit, and influence.

capabilities to enable effective planning. The roles of specialized capability professionals within IO had been clarified.[132]

Conclusion

Information operations are linked to the convergent nature of conflict doctrinally through tasks and purposes, and through information-related capabilities that affect the physical, informational, and cognitive domains. Capabilities affecting the physical domain include, but are not limited to, EW jamming assets, maneuver forces in support of IO objectives, special technical capabilities, tactical PSYOP speaker teams, public affairs journalists, and combat camera. Physical capabilities are used within the physical dimension and their effects are easily observed. Capabilities affecting the information domain include computer network operations, the spectrum of media conduits and telecommunications outlets. Cognitive affecting capabilities include PSYOP, PA, and deception-based information conduits when used to influence adversarial decision-making.

Information operations have tasks that are executed within all three of the domains of conflict. The tasks are: destroy, disrupt, degrade, deny, deceive, exploit, and influence. These tasks are linked in varying degrees to the physical, informational, and cognitive domains. Destroy is a physical dimension task.[133] Disrupt, degrade, are both

---

[132]This does not imply that specialized capability professionals are necessarily subordinate to IO planners.

[133]FM 3-13, *Information Operations,* Draft, 2-14. Author's analysis; destroy is defined as the use of lethal and nonlethal means to physically render adversary information useless or information systems ineffective unless reconstituted.

physical and informational dimension tasks.[134] Deny, deceive, exploit and influence are informational and cognitive dimension tasks.[135] Information operations could be viewed as a cognitive form of maneuver when the offensive and defensive information-related tasks and capabilities are applied to the physical, informational, and cognitive domains of conflict.[136] As a cognitive form of maneuver, US Army IO can be applied in four ways: to control information being transmitted to friendly and home audiences, the control of information into and within areas of operation and those areas affecting military operations, causing adversarial and enemy audiences to act in a manner that supports US Army operations, and to protect US Army operations."[137]

---

[134]Ibid. Author's analysis; disrupt is defined as the breaking or interrupting the flow of information between selected command and control nodes; electronic attack is identified as a common means of doing so. Degrade is defined as using nonlethal or temporary means to reduce the effectiveness or efficiency of targeted command and control systems. This may normally be done through computer attack or electronic attack.

[135]Ibid. Author's analysis; deny is the withholding of information about friendly forces, operations or situations that can be used by adversaries and enemies. Deceive is to misinform an adversary or enemy of one's actions. Exploit is to gain access to targeted command and control networks to collect information or to insert false or misleading information. Influence is to cause others to behave in a manner favorable to friendly forces.

[136]Richard Piscal, interview by Ken Crowe, Basra, Iraq, December 28, 2010; Department of the Army, Field Manual (FM) 3-90, *Tactics* (Washington, DC: Government Printing Office, January 23, 2009), chapter 3. COL Richard Piscal, the 1ID Chief of Staff during the deployment, commented that "[i]nformation operations has become a form of maneuver during this deployment, much more so than when I was here in 2003 and 2004." There are five forms of maneuver: envelopment, turning movement, infiltration, penetration, and frontal attack. The five forms of maneuver reside within the physical domain of conflict. Although not physical in nature, information can be maneuvered to achieve objectives. COL Piscal's observation implies that it would be helpful for commanders to understand the relationship between the physical and cognitive domains of conflict.

[137]Leah Armistead, *Information Warfare: Separating Hype from Reality.* (Washington, DC: Potomac Books, 2007), 21. The exact quote is "[i]t became clear to

The author defines the control of information out of an area of operations as the release of truthful and accurate messages pertaining to US Army operations to US and friendly international audiences. Sample methods for doing so are through media releases, unit sponsored social media sites, and command information programs. The author clarifies the control of information into and within areas of operations as the use of attributable-information to influence the behaviors of target audiences. Methods for doing so include leaflet and pamphlet distribution, host nation radio and television outlets, and through opinion editorials printed in local newspapers. The manipulation of information against an adversarial target audience is the use of information, disinformation, and misinformation to influence the behaviors adversarial target audiences. This can be done through the integrated use of special technical capabilities, military deception, and offensive IO. Protecting information is the guarding of and careful selection of released information to protect US Army operations, and may be done by following proper information assurance guidelines, the proper handling of intelligence, and the tailored use of talking points by US Army personnel during media engagements.[138]

Information operations began as a technical counter to the Soviet REC concept. Doctrinal transformations broadened IO's application to include the use of capabilities that affected the cognitive domain. With these changes, the tasks and purpose of IO became unclear within the US army, which created confusion as to how IO should be integrated into operations. Emerging doctrine seeks to better clarify IO and stratify its

---

warfighters that the side controlling the most information and retaining the ability to accurately manipulate and conduct an influence campaign was going to be victorious."

[138]Author's construct, to be applied to the case studies.

components to allow easier integration. The proposal of the convergent nature of conflict

construct is intended to provide the context for IO's integration during periods of

unstable peace and insurgency through the above-defined four ways, which will be used

to examine the convergent nature of conflict within the following Dhofar and Iraq case

studies.

CHAPTER 4

DHOFAR

The purpose of this chapter is to examine the actions of the Dhofari Information

Service during the Dhofari insurgency, 1970-1975, in order to understand how

information operations were integrated into the Sultan of Oman's government and the

British Army Training Team's (BATT) counterinsurgency strategy. The activities of

Dhofari Information Service during the insurgency were significant from the perspective

that they implemented what is now considered IO before the concept had been proposed.

The concept of information operations had not yet been created. Information operations

was an American doctrinal concept. The British conducted operations that would now be

considered IO as part of their PSYOP construct.[139] There was little governing doctrine for

the integration and synchronization of influence activities at that time; the Dhofar

information service performed many of the coordinating duties and responsibilities

currently executed by US Army information operations practitioners according to their

instincts and initiative. The Dhofari Information Service adapted to the operating

environment and performed those tasks deemed necessary to support the Omani

government's counterinsurgency campaign. Examining the activities of the Dhofari

Information Service provides the opportunity to compare the differences between British

---

[139]Information operations were not a concept in the early 1970s, which may
contribute to confusion as to the distinction between IO and PSYOP. Information
operations is a doctrinal concept, PSYOP is an information related capability. For the
purposes of simplicity and to write in the language of those interviewed, PSYOP will be
used to refer to all information operations related activities examined in this case study.
The doctrinal term information operations or IO, is used in the IO Doctrinal Evolution
Review and Iraq case study chapters.

and US doctrines. British influence activities had a its origins in PSYOP; American IO's origins were in electronic warfare.

This case study will examine the context of the insurgency (the physical environment and threat), the BATT PSYOP strategy, examples of operations, and operational assessments. Conclusions will be based upon the three analytical constructs developed in the previous COIN theorist review chapter.[140]

Dhofar's physical environment and the operational threat

Because of its location, Oman facilitates control of all maritime traffic moving through the Straits of Hormuz.[141] Oman is located on the southern tip of the Arabian Peninsula, bordered by Saudi Arabia to the north and the Peoples Democratic Republic of Yemen to the west.[142] Dhofar is the western-most province of Oman; physically separated from the remainder of the country by desert to the north and rough terrain to the east and northeast. The province is a thirty-seven miles long and nine miles deep coastal strip. To the immediate north of the coastal strip is the *Jebel* Plateau, which dominates the majority of the terrain of Oman and runs from the west to the east, parallel to the coast, for one hundred and fifty miles (see figure 1 and 2).[143]

---

[140]The analytical constructs are: security enables civil-military operations, both exploited by an information strategy; adaptability by the counterinsurgent is a key to success; and convergence describes the nature of conflict (past, present, and future).

[141]Ibid.

[142]Roger Cole and Richard Belfield, *SAS Operation Storm* (London: Hodder and Stoughton Ltd., 2010), 17.

[143]Becket, 175; Major General Tony Jeapes, *SAS Secret War: Operation Storm in the Middle East* (London: Greenhill Books, 2005). Major General Jeapes provides a more detailed and colorful physical description of Dhofar in chapter one of *SAS Secret War*.

Photo Removed Due to Copyright Restrictions

Figure 1. Map of Oman
Source: British Military Source Files, "Dhofar Presentation" (Briefing, United Kingdom, Date Unknown).

Photo Removed Due to Copyright Restrictions

Figure 2.   Map of Dhofar
Source: Major General Tony Jeapes, *SAS Secret War: Operation Storm in the Middle East* (London: Greenhill Books, 2005), 16.

Approximately two thirds of the province's population was located within the coastal strip.[144] The remaining population was made up of nomadic tribesmen, called *Jebalis*, who raised cattle and goats on the Jebel Plateau.[145] Islam was the predominant religion for the area.[146]

---

[144]Becket; CF20110914W0001, interview by Darrell Vaughan, London, England (September 14, 2011).

[145]Ian F. W. Beckett, "The British Counterinsurgency Campaign in Dhofar 1965-75," in *Counterinsurgency in Modern Warfare*, ed. Daniel Marston and Carter Malkasian (Oxford: Osprey Publishing, 2010), 175.

[146]CF20110914W0001, interview; CF20110912J0001, interview by Art of War Scholars Team 3, Warminster, England, September 12, 2011. Islam was the predominant faith. However, according to a former member of the Dhofari Information Service, there was seen evidence of paganism, usually expressed in terms of superstitious practices and

Inter-tribal warfare, because of the competition for resources such as grazing areas and water sources, was the norm for *Jebali* culture and prevented the establishment of a sense of national identity.[147] The loyalties of a *Jebali* were to cattle, family, and the tribe last.[148] Loyalty to the Sultan was often tenuous and would become one of the Sultan's primary objectives during the 1965 insurgency. The migratory nature of the *Jebalis* also made it difficult for them to be integrated into the larger Omani society.

Because the *Jebalis* were ethnically different from other Omanis, and the austere conditions of life on the *jebel*, they considered themselves better than other Omanis, and extended their cultural elitism towards the inhabitants of the coastal plain.[149] They lived in small tribal groups; following the herds to wherever they thought was good food and water and migrating according to the monsoon season.[150] Despite their elitists' mindset,

---

various forms of nature worship ("they worshipped trees"). For example, pork is taboo, however, mothers were seen tearing small pieces of pork, which had been encased in plastic packaging material, and placing them within a wrap around their children's waists. This practice was believed to help ward off evil spirits. The source continued by saying that the people were slightly embarrassed by their pagan practices.

[147]Cole and Belfield, 17; Tony Jeapes, *SAS Secret War: Operation Storm in the Middle East* (London: Greenhill Books, 2005), 108. As said by author Roger Cole and Belfield regarding tribal conflict, there was "a tradition of tribes feuding with their neighbors over the only three things that mattered in life: land, water, and cattle." This conflict was often expressed through honor killings. Major General Jeapes described Dhofari culture as such: the "Dhofar's social background is uncomplicated: incessant tribal warfare pursued for centuries with an unrelenting zeal."

[148]Becket, 176.

[149]CF20110914W0001, interview; CF20110912J0001, interview. This cultural elitism went both ways, from the Omanis to the Dhofaris and vice versa.

[150]Becket, 176. The monsoon season was between June and September, after which the Jebalis would move from the jebel into camps, situated within the wadis at its base.

the people on the *jebel* maintained links with the coastal settlers through both familial and trading ties.[151]

The Dhofari grievances with Sultan Said bin Taimur stemmed from a poor civil capacity infrastructure, limited means for economic prosperity, and a general distrust of the government. The conditions on the *jebel* during the 1960s were very poor. There was no public transport in or out of the province except by boat, no (improved) roads, electricity, or a postal service. There was also no means for the delivery of public information, such as newspapers, radio broadcasting or television stations. There was a lack of basic education. Poverty, due to limited economic opportunities, was high, which was further exacerbated when the Sultan expelled all Dhofaris from the army in the late 1960s.[152] These factors, coupled with a strong suspicion of the government's motives, challenged the Omani government's attempts to communicate with the *Jebalis* by causing open communication between the two groups to practically cease.[153]

---

[151]Becket, 175; CF20110914W0001, interview; CF20110912J0001, interview. Because of illiteracy within the Jebalis, the tribesmen would get people from the coast to read pamphlets to them. The Information Branch throughout the duration of the conflict exploited these links as information conduits for the passage of propaganda. The Dhofaris were also large trading tribes, with links between Aden and Oman. They traded abroad, and, many who left the country during the 1960s and later returned, had worked as far away as England. The result was a group of people who were not as mentally isolated as one might think for someone living in primitive areas.

[152]Becket, 176; CF20110914W0001, interview; Cole and Belfield, 22. Service in the army was a means for Dhofaris to earn an income. Expulsion from the Omani Army had a negative economic effect on the Jebalis. This would later have a negative effect on the Sultan's Armed Forces operating out of Salalah by not having any indigenous peoples to aid in establishing positive relationships with the Dhofari locals. The SAF was composed mostly of Baluch and northern Omani or Arabs, led by British Army officers. Many Dhofaris sought military service in other Arab states.

[153]CF20110914W0001, interview. The use of government-sponsored propaganda was difficult. This was overcome by exploitation of the informal communications

History

British involvement in Oman began in 1798 when they established a presence in Oman to protect British imperial trade interests in the Persian Gulf. By signing a defense treaty with the Sultan of Oman, the British were in a position to exploit Oman's location and control access to Persia (Iran), India and East Africa. The British signed a defense treaty with the Sultan in 1798, which gave the Sultan absolute authority over his territory while the British, when requested, provided military aid to defend the country from adversaries both within and outside.[154]

Omani wealth was originally based on the slave trade during the eighteenth and nineteenth centuries. When the slave trade ended, the country itself became increasingly impoverished, causing friction between the Sultan and the tribes of the interior.[155] The British, in an attempt to restore stability, negotiated a peace treaty that shared power between the Sultan and the ranking *Jebali* Imam. Discontent between the Dhofaris and the Sultan would continue to grow, until in the 1950s, a new Imam, Ghalib bin Ali, came to power and challenged the Sultan's authority. Ghalib facilitated two Saudi Arabian led invasions, which were repelled by the British officered Sultan's Armed Forces and the SAS, of oil rich lands along the Saudi Arabian-Omani border during the late 1950s and

---

information conduits of the tribes. Word of mouth was to be one the more reliable information conduits within the area.

[154]Cole and Belfield, 18. As stated earlier, Oman is positioned to control the Straits of Hormuz. Persia, India, and East Africa were major imperial markets at the time. Roger Cole and Belfield and Richard Belfield's book *SAS Operation Storm* provides more detail on the conflict between the British and French.

[155]Cole and Belfield, 19; CF20110914W0001, interview.

early 1960s.[156] These challenges to the Sultan's authority caused him to close the country's borders and impose heavy-handed measures that further alienated the Dhofari people from the remainder of Oman.[157] As the Dhofaris rebelled, the Sultan's actions became more repressive.

The Sultan Said bin Taimur's leadership style was his undoing. He was an autocratic ruler who had been in power since 1932. As previously stated, he controlled movement within the country, which contributed to the overall dismal condition of the Dhofaris.[158] The vast majority of the population was undereducated. There were only three state-run schools in the country, which were primarily for males and denied education beyond the primary level.[159] Medical care was mostly absent and only one hospital in the country. Ailments such as malaria, trachoma, and glaucoma, were endemic. Symbols of modernity were banned. This included medical drugs, spectacles, radios, bicycles, cigarettes, music and dancing. The situation was worsened by the failure

---

[156]Cole and Belfield, 20; CF20110914W0001, interview; CF20110914DV0001, interview. The British provided seconded and contract officers to the SAF for a number of years. The salaries for both the seconded officers and their replacements within the British military ranks were paid by the Sultan's government in addition; in essence the Omani government paid twice the salary for one man. Contract officers were released temporarily from British service and paid directly by the Omain government. They were allowed to return to British military service upon the completion of their contracts.

[157]Cole and Belfield, 19; CF20110914W0001, interview. Other tactics, such as the capping of wells combined with the restricted movement of the tribes, would often result in the deaths of Dhofaris as they starved within their houses. Actions such as these would further widen the gap between the Sultan and the Dhofaris.

[158]Becket, 176; CF20110914W0001, interview; CF20110912J0001, interview. The Sultan restricted movement of people from their homes, denying them of access to water and food, resulting in deaths by dehydration and starvation.

[159]Becket 176; CF20110914W0001, interview.

of the Sultan to use oil revenues to improve the quality of life of the Omanis.[160] Yemeni communists, realizing how the Sultan's repressive behavior provided fertile territory for recruitment and a means to spread their ideology within the region, saw the opportunity to expand their influence into Oman.[161]

The Dhofari insurgency began in 1965 when *Jebali* dissidents met at the First Congress.[162] The most dominant group was the Dhofar Liberation Front (DLF), formed by Mussalim bin Nufl[163] of the Al-Kathari sub-group of the Bait Kathir-Jebelli in the early 1960s.[164] It was a nationalist organization. Training and funding to the organization had been provided by Saudi Arabia until the late 1960s, when the Chinese, Soviet Union and Iraq then provided support.[165]

The communists took control of the DLF during the Second Congress in 1967. The nationalist followers of bin Nufl were ousted from DLF leadership in 1968, and the organization re-named itself the Popular Front for the Liberation of the Occupied Arabian

---

[160]Becket 176; CF20110914W0001, interview; CF20110912J0001, interview.

[161]Becket, 177. Yemen fell to the communists in 1967.

[162]Cole and Belfield, 21.

[163]Jeapes, 57. Bin Nufl would be instrumental in the formation of the first *firqat*, Firqat Salahadin.

[164]Becket, 177.

[165]Ibid., 178. Justification for this support came from a long-standing territorial dispute over the Buraimi area of Oman. The British officered Trucial Oman Scouts defeated a Saudi supported incursion into this area in 1955.The DLF also suffered a serious setback in leadership when bin Nufl was seriously wounded during this time period.

Gulf.[166] The organization would have two further name changes, one in 1971 to the

Popular Front for the Liberation of Oman and the Arabian Gulf (PFLOAG) and the last to

the Popular Front for the Liberation of Oman (PFLO) in 1974.[167]

The insurgents used the takeover of the DLF to advance their agenda, which

included breaking up Omani tribalism, ending Western imperialism, and creating a

communist state.[168] The PFLOAG narrative espoused a popular movement led by 'poor

classes, such as farmers, workers, soldiers, and revolutionary intellectuals with the

purpose of destroying the imperialist presence in all its forms, military, economic and

political."[169] The PFLOAG, operating from safe havens in Yemen, provided weapons and

money, and began a mass indoctrination program that included the use of child soldiers,

the establishment of schools, civil capacity projects on the jebel, and popular education in

communist theory.[170] The PFLOAG also expanded its military capabilities.

---

[166]Cole and Belfield, 22,178.

[167]Ibid. For the sake of consistency, the organization will be referred to as PFLOAG for the remainder of this chapter.

[168]Becket, 178. Becket used Marxist and communist synonymously. For simplicity, communism and its derivatives will be used.

[169]Cole and Belfield, 21; CF20110914W0001, interview; CF20110912J0001, interview. PFLOAG's narrative did not resonate with many *Jebalis* for two reasons: those types of individuals and social classes did not exist amongst the Dhofaris, and the forced rejection of Islam upon the populace. The Dhofaris were simple herdsmen who wanted liberation from an autocratic leader instead of a social revolution. Also, the PFLOAG banned and punished Islamic worship.

[170]Becket, 178; Cole and Belfield, 21, 23. In Rakhuyt, insurgents executed the wali (the local representative of the Sultan) and massacred all of the male inhabitants. Children were deprived of food and water until they renounced Islam. Once that had occurred, they were fed, accompanied with the message that the PFLOAG was feeding them, not Allah.

The communists through PFLOAG military forces established control of the *jebel.* By 1970, the PFLOAG was able to field two thousand active insurgents in the People's Liberation Army, and three thousand men in the part-time *Jebali* militia. The insurgents, outnumbering the Sultan's Armed Forces (SAF) and having secure supply lines to Yemen, were able to operate freely, and used intimidation and death squads to enforce their control.[171] Oman was close to losing the insurgency when the British became involved in 1970.

British involvement in the campaign

The Sultan's son, Qaboos, dethroned his father in 1970 and requested aid from the British.[172] The British were motivated by the desire to stop the spread of communism in the Middle East, but support was not popular in the United Kingdom. The fall of the British colony of Aden and British supported South Arabia to a communist government, later renamed the People's Democratic Republic of Yemen, was viewed as part of the communist domino effect of the 1960s. Oman was seen as a proxy war, similar to Laos, Vietnam, and Yemen, between the communist powers and the United States and the United Kingdom.[173]

---

[171]Becket, 178. Death squads were called *idaarat.*

[172]CF20110914DV0001, interview by Art of War Scholars Team 3, Warminster, England, September 14, 2011; CF20110914W0001, interview; CF20110912J0001, interview. Qaboos was a graduate from the Britain's Royal Military Academy, Sandhurst. After completing his education and returning to Oman, his father placed him on house arrest. Qaboos led a bloodless coup, which was more than likely supported by the British. More information on the coup is provided by MG Jeapes in *SAS Secret War.*

[173]Ibid., 22.

Sultan Qaboos inherited the troubles created by his father. Sultan Taimur had had no campaign plan with which to fight PFLOAG. Modernization of the SAF had begun by this time, but SAF equipment as a whole was not adequate for operations on the *jebel*.[174] The Sultan had refused to make any political concessions towards the *Jebalis* and publicly stated he wanted the Dhofaris destroyed.[175] The PFLOAG, although as unpopular as the Sultan, had presence on the *jebel*. The SAF, restricted to the villages of Salalah, Taqa and Mirbat, would make short-term forays onto the plateau, but then leave soon after operations were completed creating the perception that the Sultan was not committed to *jebel* security. Upon assuming the throne, Sultan Qaboos immediately set about correcting the situation.

Strategy and operations

British military officers assigned to the Sultan's Armed Forces formulated a strategy for fighting the insurgency provided three guiding principles. First, there needed to be strong policies for the development and rehabilitation of essential services by the government. Second, early successes by the Sultan's forces needed to be visible to the *Jebalis*. Finally, the government needed to consider the political aspects of any operation.[176] These three point were operationalized through the Watts Plan.

---

[174]CF20110912J0001, interview; CF20110913C0001, interview; CF20110914DV0001, interview; CF20110914W0001, interview. The SAF were receiving helicopters, modern rifles, and Strikemaster aircraft. They needed uniforms that blended with the terrain and boots durable enough for operations on the rocky *jebel*.

[175]Becket, 179.

[176]Becket, 180. A paraphrase of Brigadier John Graham, then commander of the Dhofar Brigade, quoted by Becket.

The SAS commanding officer, Lieutenant Colonel John Watts, and his operations

officer, Major Peter de la Billiere developed the counterinsurgency strategy, called the

'Watts Plan'. The Watts Plan had five lines of effort, or 'fronts'. The first was the

identification of areas of collection and collation of intelligence, controlled by an

established intelligence cell. The second was medical assistance to the *Jebalis* provided

by a medical officer and supported by SAS medics. The third was veterinary facilities for

the improvement of the *Jebali* cattle stock administered by a veterinary officer. The

fourth was the use of indigenous peoples, the Dhofaris, directly involved in their own

defense, fighting for the Sultan. The fifth was the creation of an information service to

disseminate government views to the populace.[177] The plan addressed both short and

long-term objectives for the Omani government; short-term measures were to bring

immediate relief to the *Jebalis* until the Omani government was capable of assuming the

tasks, and long-term measures were intended to demonstrate commitment to the civil

development of Dhofar.[178]

Sultan Qaboos quickly acted upon the development and rehabilitation of essential

services by lifting movement restrictions, releasing political prisoners, and freeing

slaves.[179] He announced a development plan, funded by oil revenues, which included

---

[177]Becket, 180; Jeapes, 32-33; CF20110914W0001, interview.

[178]Becket, 180.

[179]Becket, 179; CF20110914W0001, interview. Sultan Qaboos regarded the freed slaves as royal servants and provided jobs to the community within Salalah. A source reported that a freed slave had requested to join, and was accepted into, the information service. Sultan Qaboos denied the individual permission to join the organization, instead insisting that he would provide for his subjects and found equally suitable employment elsewhere within his administration.

new schools, clinics, housing, and a communications infrastructure. To implement his plan, Education, Health, Interior, and Justice Ministries were formed. Sultan Qaboos, seeking local and international support, joined Oman in the United Nations and the Arab League and, as previously mentioned, formally requested assistance from the British to assist in defeating the PFLOAG.[180] British assistance would come in the form of a detachment of the 22 Special Air Squadron (SAS).

Support to Oman was not popular with the British government and citizenry. In the late 1960s, the United Kingdom had been forced from Aden and was itself involved in a resource intensive counterinsurgency in Northern Ireland. Approval for support was based upon the recognized need by the British to halt communist expansion and protect the oil routes through the Straits of Hormuz.[181] Britain agreed to provide support based upon two stipulations: it would be an economy of effort operation using a small force from the SAS, and that knowledge of the operation would be kept as secret as long possible.[182]

The British government restricted support to being a small group of specialists and advisers who were ultimately responsible to the Sultan. The SAS provided fifty-man teams, named British Army Training Teams (BATTs) as advisers, along with support personnel drawn from the RAF Regiment, the Royal Artillery, the Royal Signals, the

---

[180]Becket, 179; Jeapes, 17-33. Jeapes provides a detailed account of the issues facing Sultan Qaboos as he assumed power.

[181]Ibid.

[182]CF20110912J0001, interview; CF20110914DV0001, interview; CF20110914W0001, interview.

Royal Engineers, and a field surgical team. British forces were based out of the Salalah airfield[183]

Implementation of the Watts Plan: The information service

In 1970, the information service was a 'team' of one person, an SAS corporal with a penchant for PSYOP and a small degree of training received prior to his deployment to Dhofar. However, there was not much PSYOP doctrine for the information section to base their operations upon.[184] The information service did not have a doctrinal task description or clearly defined tasks. Instead, the members of the team were self-guided in their mission objectives. The information service identified the tasks they needed to perform and the resources needed to accomplish those tasks.

The Dhofari Information Service coordinated and executed their operations through an informal, relationship based process. For example, strong interpersonal relationships were established with members of the Dhofari government offices who were able to provide advice and needed equipment, such as printing presses and broadcast equipment.[185] The same was true between the information service and the other

---

[183]Becket, 180.

[184]Ibid; CF20110914W0001, interview. PSYOP was not a clearly defined discipline for the British military at that time. Training was based off of West German military tactics, techniques, and procedures. Investment in PSYOP training and development would remain inconsistent. According to the source, the term did not have a great deal of meaning, and serious thought to the discipline from the British military wouldn't be given again until Bosnia. Jeapes echoed this viewpoint (and confusion) when he said in *SAS Secret War*, page 36, "[t]he whole subject of information services is one bedeviled by emotive phrases and misunderstanding" and that the phrase psychological operations implied brain washing and lies.

[185]Jeapes, 36; CF20110914W0001, interview. Jeapes described him as an "average SAS corporal but at information services he was brilliant."

British military forces in Dhofar. For example, the information service would provide aerial photography support to the RAF in exchange for leaflet drops.[186] Later on in the campaign, the information service would grow to include over one hundred fifty personnel and Army Information Teams (AIT) would also be assigned from the British military.

Army Information Teams were fifteen-man teams under the supervision of an officer and a non-commissioned officer, equipped with loudspeaker mounted cargo trucks. The AITs were very similar to the Tactical PSYOP Speaker Teams currently used by the US Army. The members of the AITs were from other occupational specialties, selected from disparate units and assembled for the mission, and much like the information service corporal, received a brief amount of PSYOP training before arriving in theater.[187]

In addition to performing the duties of message distribution, the AITs also took photographs while on patrol, which were used for both propaganda purposes and to show progress to the military and governmental leadership. They also had access to other assets, such as speaker-mounted aircraft called the Sky Shout system.[188]

The information service had three goals: to support the military operational aims, to assist in the military and political defeat of the dissidents, and to persuade the

---

[186]CF20110914W0001, interview. Another example is when he acquired two hundred pairs of boots for Army units through an engagement with a visiting military official.

[187]CF20110914W0001, interview.

[188]CF20110912J0001, interview; CF20110913C0001, interview; CF20110914DV0001, interview; CF20110914W0001, interview. Due to technical problems, this capability was not used often.

population of the integrity of the Sultan's government. These aims were operationalized through three LOEs.[189]

The first LOE was an integrated hearts and minds campaign executed by the BATTs and CATs as they circulated through safe villages demonstrating security and giving both medical support and veterinary assistance. These efforts were synchronized with the information service to ensure there were no compromises in operations.[190] The second LOE was an information campaign that communicated that the new government was both different and better than the old. The final LOE, as mentioned previously, was the encouragement of *adoo* fighters to surrender.[191]

The information service, although being British soldiers, knew that they were representing Sultan Qaboos's government not Britain's. The communications strategy was designed to promote the primacy of the Sultan with consistent messaging of the government party narrative while undermining the legitimacy of PFLOAG. Emphasis was placed on promoting the character of the Sultan, building a sense of nationalism, ensuring that the populace knew that the government was responsible for the distribution of wealth and that everyone was getting the share of wealth they were entitled to.[192]

As stated previously, the primacy of the Sultan was consistently emphasized. He was portrayed as a caring monarch and as a religious man who worked for Islam.

---

[189]CF20110914W0001, interview.

[190]Ibid.

[191]Ibid.

[192]CF20110914W0001, interview. The irony of the wealth sharing initiative of the government is its similarity to communism, the platform that PFLOAG based their ideology upon.

Stressing Sultan Qaboos's religious nature was important to help undermine the

communists' anti-God rhetoric. Promoting the Sultan and his symbols of office, such as

his cap badge,[193] gave legitimacy to the government and encouraged nationalism. For

example, popular input was allowed for the re-design of the national flag. The old flag,

under Taimur, was solid red. The new flag had a solid red border on the left with the

national symbol at the top, and three colored stripes, white, red, and green, on the left.

The creation of the new flag symbolized change within the country, symbolism that was

also exploited by the information service.[194]

Information service messages stressed that the government would provide for the

people, that everything the government did was perfect, and that the new Sultan was

better than the old and what he was providing was better than what the *Jebalis* had had

before.[195] Delegitimizing the PFLOAG was facilitated by exploiting the communists'

underestimation of the importance of Islam to the Dhofaris and their intimidation

tactics.[196]

The use of slogans was important, especially when used to delegitimize the

PFLOAG. Slogans that were religious in nature, such as 'The Hand of God Destroys

Communism' (see Figure 2), resonated with the Dhofaris against PFLOAG. Another,

'Freedom is Our Aim, and Islam is Our Way', became popular with both the Dhofaris

---

[193]The cap badge, was composed of crossed swords with a curved Khanjar knife (the traditional dagger of Oman) on top would become the national symbol.

[194]CF20110914W0001, interview.

[195]Ibid.

[196]Cole and Belfield, 24.

and the BATT leadership. It linked freedom, Islam, and the government, and was used at the end of every day's radio broadcast and incorporated into leaflets. According to Jeapes, "[y]ears later, I was assured by a Dhofari it was an old Dhofari saying whose origins were lost in antiquity."[197]

Photo Removed Due to Copyright Restrictions

Figure 3.   Sample PSYOP leaflet graphic
Source: Dhofari Information Service, "The Hand of God Destroys Communism," http://en.wikipedia.org/wiki/File:Hand_of_God.jpg (accessed November 16, 2011).

Sultan Qaboos and the BATT leadership decided early on to protect the Sultan's legitimacy by using only use truthful messages.[198] The Sultan insisted on fair and balanced reporting by requiring that all perspectives and viewpoints be presented in the

---

[197]Jeapes, 60.

[198]CF20110912J0001, interview; CF20110914W0001, interview.

news. For example, newspapers were spreading stories of Muslim mosques being burned in a neighboring country. The truth of the story was that the burnings were reprisals to other actions to include the burning of Christian churches in the same communities. In order for the stories to be run in the Omani newspaper, both sides of the reprisal burnings had to be presented.[199] This proved a reliable counter-narrative to PFLOAG's negative government ideology; especially after a radio service had been established. The *Jebali* did not trust radio Aden, the source of PFLOAG radio propaganda.[200]

Information conduits to the Dhofaris were initially limited due to an undeveloped Omani communications infrastructure. The information service used six primary information conduits to its target audiences: notice boards, leaflets, word of mouth, newspapers, radio, and television. Notice boards were placed in locations where people congregated, such as checkpoints at the entrances to Salalah or Mirbat. Information would be posted on the boards, and as people waited to be cleared for entry into the towns, a literate Dhofari would be on-hand to read the notices to interested parties.[201]

The Dhofari Information Service implemented a leaflet campaign that included the use of pro-government and Islam messages and imagery, pictures of government sponsored civil capacity projects, and encouragement to join the government with instructions on how to do so. The leaflets did not directly argue against the PFLOAG narrative. Instead, imagery such as pictures of two bushes, one with leaves and 'Islam'

---

[199]CF20110914W0001, interview.

[200]Becket, 183.

[201]CF20110914W0001, interview.

71

written under it, and one without leaves and 'Communism' written under it were used.[202] Instructions on how to join the government was so effective that defecting *adoo* at times thought they had to have a leaflet in hand in order to do so.[203] Confirmation of the truthfulness of the leaflets' messages were facilitated by word of mouth amongst the Dhofaris, as verification spread along family lines, eventually reaching the *adoo* camps.[204]

The Dhofari Information Service conducted leaflet drops at night and used culturally appropriate imagery and slogans. The use of host nation citizens to help design the products was important.[205] Originally, translators from the Intelligence Service were used. Their insistence on using proper Arabic compromised information service products. The Dhofari Information Service found that using local Dhofaris, writing in their imperfect but locally recognized Arabic, were the most effective. Attention to the materials used was also important. Leaflets had to be produced on low quality paper. High quality paper contained watermarks, which were indicators that the leaflets originated with the British instead of the Omanis.[206]

Night delivery of leaflets also played upon the superstitious nature of the *Jebalis*. Reportedly, a leaflet landed on the head of an *adoo* who was relieving himself in the

---

[202]CF20110914W0001, interview; CF20110912J0001, interview.

[203]CF20110914W0001, interview.

[204]Ibid.

[205]This is a common practice in modern operations also. Omani ex-patriots were instrumental in the development of information service PSYOP products.

[206]CF20110914W0001, interview.

early morning. The *adoo* took the leaflet landing on him as a sign from God and defected shortly thereafter.[207]

The information service originated Oman's first newspaper, radio, and television station.[208] These information conduits provided access to the larger Arab community and aided in creating a sense of belonging to the Arab world. The Omanis wanted to hear about themselves in the international media, and the Sultan's insistence on fairness in reporting increased government legitimacy and improved relationships with neighboring countries.[209] These information conduits also allowed for the information service to act quickly on events, such as reporting on wrecked aircraft, which could be manipulated by the PFLOAG. There were several aircraft accidents due to human error that could have been claimed by the PFLOAG as successful attacks.[210] By having immediate access via the media outlets and an established reputation for honesty and fairness, the Omani government was able to deny the PFLOAG from being able to use those events to promote their narrative.[211]

In the case of radio possession, the BATT quickly adapted to heavy-handed PFLOAG tactics. The government originally provided small radios to the *Jebali*. The *adoo* confiscated and destroyed the radios when found on *Jebali* persons. The

---

[207]Ibid.

[208]Ibid.. The name of the newspaper was *Al Watan*.

[209]Ibid.

[210]Ibid.

[211]Jeapes, 36. *Radio Dhofar* always told the truth in order to protect the legitimacy of the Omani government.

government then began to sell the radios to the *Jebali*, increasing their value from something that had been given to them to a personal possession that had cost them money.[212] The *Jebali* became resentful when the *adoo* destroyed their radios. Selling the radios to the *Jebali* was an intentional exploitation with the purpose of eroding support to the PFLOAG.[213]

The information service eventually became the Ministry of Information (MoI) and assumed responsibility for managing the media and important visitors. The Ministry of Information consistently worked to establish positive relationships with members of the media and at times had journalists on retainer who would write favorable stories about Oman and the British forces.[214] Journalist movement was tightly controlled. When providing tours of the *jebel*, journalists were given the perception of freedom of

---

[212]The personal investment of the host nation population is important. The providing of radios to the Dhofaris was 'nice', but had no real value at first because the radios came at no expense. This is similar to the providing of civil capacity projects by the US government today. Building a school is 'nice', but if the school has no value to the populace because it came with no personal expense, then it has little lasting value. If it is destroyed by an adversary, so be it, the community returns to the status quo of before the school was built. The provision of services for free also helps create a sense of entitlement that may not be justified, such as when the Iraqis asked what had the Americans done for them lately (chapter 6). However, if the community has to invest in the project in some way, such as financially or physically, then the value of the project increases dramatically. This provides perspective of how to implement a 'Hearts and Minds' strategy. Does the government want compliance (Galula's carrot or stick application), or does the government want to placate the masses (a 'please like me' approach)? McCuen stated that mobilizing the masses required more than just winning the people over. They needed to realize that they had a vested interest in the success of the government. Having a vested interest in the services provided is more enduring than 'liking' the government.

[213]Jeapes, 37; CF20110914W0001, interview.

[214]CF20110914W0001, interview. The retainer fee was five thousand pounds per year.

74

movement as they were escorted to locations chosen by the Ministry of Information. The MoI provided unique opportunities, such as allowing a journalist to lay claim to riding in the first vehicle to travel along a newly opened road on the *jebel* that resulted in a favorable article reporting on the on-going development of Oman. A '60 Minutes' news team, after having been treated to a catered luncheon overlooking two border forts along the Yemen-Omani border, reportedly produced an hour-long special on the Sultan's development of the country. The MoI ensured that all visitors left the country with the story that the Sultan wanted told.

The BATT and the information service conducted deception operations. Military deception was used during Operation Jaguar, a major offensive operation conducted in October 1971, to protect the details of the timing of the operation from the *adoo*. Hints were dropped in casual conversation identifying a false location for the attack two weeks in advance. The day prior to the operation, two *firqat* drew attention away from the main advance by conducting a movement in the opposite direction from the attack.[215] A similar operation was conducted in 1973 to draw attention away from the Hornbeam Line to protect the positioning of Iranian Special Forces.[216]

Information services conducted deception operations of a more covert nature. For example, after having established a postal system on the *jebal*, it was discovered that *adoo* were using the drop boxes to mail plans to safe havens in Aden.[217] This provided a

---

[215]Jeapes, 136. This is a ruse most commonly associated with Military Deception. Jeapes provides greater detail on Operation Jaguar in chapter 8, *SAS Secret War*.

[216]Ibid, 164-165. Information service participation in these MILDEC initiatives were minimal; the BATT leadership instead planned them.

[217]CF20110914W0001, interview.

valuable means for the interception of intelligence. Intercepted messages from the *adoo* allowed for the fabrication of false messages that were re-inserted into the *adoo* network. In one instance, an *adoo* turned himself in with a letter from his previous *adoo* cell leader. His former leadership wrote that the man was unreliable and that his gaining *adoo* cell was to kill him. This letter provided two opportunities for exploitation. It had the seal of the adoo on it, which was duplicated and used to create messages that claimed other PFLOAG members had betrayed their colleagues and should be disposed of. This deception resulted in the assassinations of several *adoo* members.[218] The contents of the letter were also used to discredit the PFLOAG.

Another deception involved the use of fake parachutist dummies, similar to those used during the D Day invasion of World War Two. They were small, sand bag dummies and plywood boards with small explosives attached in parachute harnesses. The dummies resembled human beings from afar and the plywood boards sounded like small arms fire when they landed. These were used to support the story that the Sultan had formed an elite parachute regiment that he intended to use against the *adoo*.[219]

Deception was also used to influence international perceptions. Oman wanted to say to the United Nations that Yemen was an evil country and had murdered their own people and left their bodies in the street. Photographic evidence was provided showing bodies littering the streets of Yemeni villages. The photographs were actually of Omani men, wrapped in blankets and sleeping in the streets of small Omani villages, during

---

[218]CF20110914W0001, interview.

[219]CF20110914W0001, interview. OPSEC was maintained by using trusted personnel to clean the landing zone afterwards.

Ramadan, a common practice during that time of the year. The photographs were given as evidence to the United Nations and had the desired effect.[220]

Implementation of the Watts Plan: The intelligence service

The intelligence cell performed the functions of collecting and assessing information, much like the duties performed by most military intelligence elements. The intelligence action of note in regard to the Dhofar insurgency was the handling of surrendered *adoo*[221], called Surrendered Enemy Person (SEPs). The majority of intelligence collected from the SEPs was of a military nature. The Omani Intelligence Service at Salalah conducted interrogation of the SEPs, which initially created challenges with the sharing of information.[222] The SEPs were willing to provide intelligence because of their treatment; they were treated more as prodigal sons than captured enemy fighters. Leaflet drops by the information service emphasized that enemy fighters would not be tortured if they turned themselves in to the Sultan and never used the word surrender in reference to the SEPs. The SEPs were treated with dignity and honor, and interrogation initially conducted by the *firqat* and BATTs, more closely resembled a conversation conducted with family and friends over tea and cigarettes.[223]

---

[220]Ibid. The information service, and later the Ministry of Information, had to be creative and do things on the cheap.

[221]CF20110912J0001, interview; CF20110913C0001, interview; CF20110914DV0001, interview; CF20110914W0001, interview. *Adoo* was what the insurgents were called by the BATTs. It means 'enemy', and was deliberately used to avoid giving legitimacy to the PFLOAG.

[222]Becket, 182. This issue would be corrected by 1974.

[223]CF20110912J0001, interview; CF20110913C0001, interview; CF20110914DV0001, interview; CF20110914W0001, interview. Firqat were the

Implementation of the Watts Plan: The Civil Action Teams

Medical and veterinary services were provided through an integrated civil capacity development effort. The Civil Action Teams (CATs), companion elements to the BATTs, provided support with four-person teams consisting of a medical orderly, a schoolmaster, a shopkeeper, and a team leader.[224] The CATs established two clinics at Taqa and Mirbat, which were visited regularly by the BATT medical officer.[225] Veterinarians were attached to the CATs, and provided both veterinary care and breeding programs to improve cattle stocks.

The CAT strategy was to create a track (road) to a local government center and sink a well attracting local people and livestock. Educational and medical facilities would follow. Veterinary facilities would then shortly thereafter be established for the purposes of providing medical care to livestock and improving the breeding stock. Markets would become established, and the settlements would eventually become self-sufficient.

---

indigenous military forces created in support of the fourth front. These were tribal based organizations, of which the first, *Firqat Salahadin*, failed because of the inter-tribal rivalries between its members. This integrated approach of accepting and safeguarding the SEPs, which facilitated their willingness to defect and cooperation with the Sultan's forces, exploited by an information LOE, is an example of the convergent nature of the conflict in Dhofar, which contributed greatly to both intelligence collection and provided information conduits for future information service operations.More information on the firqat can be found in Jeapes' *SAS Secret War*, Cole and Belfield's *SAS Operation Storm*, O'Neill's "Revolutionary War in Oman," and Price's *Oman: Insurgency and Development.*

[224]Becket, 182, 185. Originally these personnel were provided by the BATTs, but would later become resourced from the Omani government. As the Omani government became capable of assuming more responsibilities, Omanis would replace the BATT soldiers providing veterinary services, and schoolteachers and nurses would come from other Arab nations, such as Egypt, Lebanon, or Jordan.

[225]Becket, 182; Jeapes, 35.

Initially, the Omani government had trouble keeping pace with SAF successes; however, the Civil Aid Department was formed as the capacity to govern improved.[226]

The Civil Aid Department was established in 1973 and assumed the responsibilities of providing CAT support. As areas were cleared, the Civil Aid Department provided prefabricated buildings that were used as schools, clinics, and shops. In November 1974, eleven wells had been established on the *jebel*; that number was increased to thirty-five by June 1975, along with one hundred fifty miles of motorable track. These initiatives were important in creating a vested interest for the *Jebalis* in the Sultan.[227]

Support to the Sultan from the Dhofaris was asked for in exchange for water wells and other services.[228] The wells demonstrated commitment from the government to the *Jebalis*, improved the quality of life for the *Jebalis* and their livestock, and created markets that increased their personal wealth. Support given from a village to the *adoo* meant losing those assets. The use of this tactic, and the clearly demonstrated improvement of the lives of the *Jebalis*, caused the *Jebalis* to become more supportive of Sultan Qaboos than the PFLOAG. The delivery of essential services alone was not enough, though, to generate continued support to the government; security on the *jebel*

---

[226]Becket, 182. Wells were established in areas with a high likelihood of having water and able to sustain a semi-permanent population. Eventually, as the Omani capacity to govern improved, the Dhofar Development Committee would be formed to oversee the development of basic requirements: roads, schools, clinic, mosques, and wells.

[227]Ibid., 185. It is also worth noting that CAT provided medical support was also an effective way to collect intelligence and pass information.

[228]Jeapes, 142.

was needed. "It is important to emphasize, of course, that it was not possible even to begin to establish CATs on the *jebel* while it remained in the hands of PFLOAG."[229]

The CAT strategy provided an example of the relationship between security, civil-capacity programs, and a communications strategy. Security had to be provided to the *Jebalis*, especially after they had decided to become semi-settled in an area that could have possibly facilitated their being more easily targeted by the *adoo*. Civil capacity projects both improved the quality of life of the *Jebalis* while demonstrating a commitment of the Sultan to care for the Dhofaris. The information service exploited this by emphasizing that 'these good things' came from the Sultan. The result was the establishment of small *Jebali* settlements with a vested interest in the success of the Sultan. Security enabled civil capacity, with successes from both exploited by a communications strategy.[230]

Implementation of the Watts Plan: Security

The SAF,[231] stationed out of the garrison in Salalah, and the *firqat*, provided security.[232] The SAF were the conventional military forces of the Sultan, led by British

---

[229]Ibid.

[230]The author's assessment; the information service's communications strategy will be covered in greater detail later in the chapter.

[231]CF20110912J0001, interview; CF20110913C0001, interview; CF20110914DV0001, interview; CF20110914W0001, interview. Jordan, Iran, and the United Arab Emirates also provided military support.

[232]See Jeapes's *SAS Secret War*, Cole and Belfield's *SAS Storm*, Gardiner's *In the Service of the Sultan*, and Ray's *Dangerous Frontiers* for more in-depth coverage of the *firqat* and the SAF. The roles of both are well documented within these, and other, sources. Not being the focus of this chapter, reference to both will be made as it pertains to the operations of the information service.

officers, and the *firqat* were indigenous, militia forces raised from the *Jebalis* tasked with aiding the SAF and providing security on the *jebel*. The *firqat* were eventually further empowered and allowed to participate in the governing of tribal areas and the selection of government centers which was important in determining the location of CAT wells. The creation of the *firqats* psychologically enabled the spread of the Sultan's narrative throughout the *jebel*. Families were split across both the *firqat* and the *adoo*, with communications between the groups occurring regularly. Coupled with the PSYOP efforts of the information service, confirmation of the fulfilled promises of the Sultan by family members encouraged *adoo* defection to the Sultan.[233]

Conclusion

The relationship between security, civil capacity operations, and the information environment was evidenced throughout the Dhofar campaign. The Jebalis had to be convinced of the Sultan's commitment to security, the equitable distribution of wealth, and the delivery of essential service, and the linking of those activities to a psychological affect was accomplished through the exploitation of events within the information environment.

Prior to 1970, the *adoo* controlled the *jebel*. Excursions from the SAF, although successful in the sense that they were able to overcome the *adoo* militarily, did not remain on the *jebel* long enough to prevent the *adoo* from returning. The SAF was initially underequipped, unprepared to conduct long duration operations, and was not

---

[233]CF20110914W0001, interview.

adapted to build successful relationships with the *Jebalis*.[234] The *adoo* were in the position to continue exerting their influence through both familial ties and with coercive measures, such as intimidation and the use of death squads. Paraphrasing COIN theorists David Galula, the situation could easily be expressed through his two questions: who can hurt me now; and who remains to either hurt or help me later?[235]

The turning point for security was the establishment of the *firqat* militias, which were used to provide permanent security to the *jebal*. This practice is common in counterinsurgency campaigns, being similar to the use of local militias to protect villages during the Malayan Emergency, the creation of a constabulary during the Philippine insurgency, and the Sons of Iraq during Operation Iraqi Freedom. The significance of security was that its presence helped confirm the Sultan's promise to take care of the *Jebalis*, and provided noticeable evidence of success that was used to persuade the Dhofaris to support Qaboos. As Major General Jeapes stated, the "civilians were not going to climb off the fence until they were sure which side would win."[236]

CAT operations were enabled by improved security on the *jebel*. Their operations included providing wells, medical and veterinary care, education, and opportunities to create wealth to the tribes. These operations provided physical proof of the Sultan's commitment to the *Jebalis*, and demonstrated that the *adoo* were not all-powerful. This relationship serves to emphasize the link between security and civil capacity operations.

---

[234] CF20110912J0001, interview; CF20110913C0001, interview; CF20110914DV0001, interview; CF20110914W0001, interview.

[235] Previously cited in chapter 2, 18.

[236] Jeapes, 141.

Exploitation of security and civil capacity success was provided by the Dhofari information service's communications plan.[237]

The information service informed Dhofari, Omani, and international audiences of the successes of Sultan Qaboos's reforms. Both the British and the Sultan tightly controlled information traveling outside of the country. Visitors were not lied to, but their movements were controlled and events were presented to them in a manner favorable to Sultan Qaboos.[238]

The information service delegitimized the PFLOAG through a message strategy distributed through leaflets, radio, and television broadcasts, and spread by word of mouth within the tribes; governmental success was used to emphasize the greatness of the Sultan, and any failure was downplayed as an unfortunate event and a minor setback. The information service widely advertised successful security and civil capacity operations to

---

[237]CF20110912J0001, interview; CF20110913C0001, interview; CF20110914DV0001, interview; CF20110914W0001, interview. Author's assessment based upon readings and interviews of Dhofar campaign participants.

[238]It is possible to do the same in modern operations, however, because of the potentially high degree of transparency of operations, extra measures would have to be taken to safeguard both operations and the legitimacy of the government (and military). Development of a plan to manage the unforeseen consequences of an operation is a prudent measure of any modern military organization. With the prevalence of cellular communications in most countries and the subsequent ability to both manipulate and disseminate information nearly instantaneously, any government organization needs to be prepared to act in anticipation of unforeseen events. Controlling the movement of most people can be accomplished through the application of proper OPSEC measures, which are easily justified by stressing the operational requirement to protect military operations. Dependent upon the context of the conflict in question, it is US military policy to either truthfully report events to target audiences, or restrict reporting based upon OPSEC guidelines.

the Jebali, which supported by visual evidence in the form of photographs and through SEP personal accounts, and verified by word of mouth between family members.[239]

Civil capacity projects provided the physical proof that the government was taking an active hand in addressing the grievances of the populace, and improved security was the physical means of protecting civil capacity projects and building confidence in the abilities of the government. Without security, the civil capacity and communications initiatives were likely to fail.[240]

The BATT forces were adaptive in their execution of the Dhofar campaign. Three examples were the formation of the *firqat*, the creation of the information service, and the SEP treatment policy.

The use of host nation people to provide for their own security was a British COIN strategy.[241] The evidence for adaption in the case of the Dhofar campaign is in the final structure and composition of the *firqat*. The *firqat* were originally conceptualized through a Western cultural perspective as being multi-tribal in composition, which would become a failure for the BATTs. The *Firqat Salahadin* fractured due to inter-tribal rivalries, causing the BATTS to form future firqats along tribal lines. The use of indigenous troops as a militia was not an original tactic; however, learning from the

---

[239]Ibid.

[240]Ibid.

[241]For example, host nation militias were used by the British during the Malayan Emergency.

mistake of disregarding cultural norms, and then re-initiating the strategy is evidence of adaptability.[242]

Identifying the need for a means to tell the government's narrative to the Dhofaris was a progressive move for the BATTs. Lieutenant Colonel Watts planned for an information service to execute the PSYOP campaign. The selection of individuals with a cognitive inclination for PSYOP, providing the necessary training to them to execute their duties, and then utilizing their experiences to train the AITs and future British PSYOP practitioners was evidence of adaptability.[243] The information service functioned through personal relationships and capitalizing on events as they presented themselves. The use of men sleeping in the streets to create the impression that Yemen was killing her people was an example. The use of pictures of bushes with and without leaves to visually support Islam and counter communism was another. Using captured enemy correspondences to disrupt the *adoo* and cause internal assassinations is yet another example.

The information service was effective in adapting to events within the operating environment.[244] The members of the information service were also open to advice given by cultural experts and implemented that advice into their PSYOP products. The ability to learn is an indicator of adaptability.[245]

---

[242] Author's assessment.

[243] CF20110914W0001, interview; author's assessment.

[244] CF20110914W0001, interview; author's assessment.

[245] Another historical example is the British creation of a jungle warfare school used to prepare military units for action in Malaya.

The SEP treatment policy is another example of adaptability. The SEPs were not treated as prisoners but as prodigal sons returning to their families. This treatment was not an issue with the *firqat*, but did require careful monitoring of both the BATT members and the SAF. Treating the SEPs as guests was difficult for many members of the SAF and BATTs who did not have familial ties to the *adoo*. This was made more difficult because of human nature. Many SEPs had been in combat with the BATTs and SAF prior to their defection. It is understandable how it may have been difficult for one of those soldiers to treat someone who was just trying to kill them as a friend, requiring the need for a strictly monitored and enforced SEP treatment policy. The SEP policy was justified by emphasizing that by not killing or mistreating the SEPs, the Sultan's narrative was being spread throughout the *adoo,* which in turn encouraged more *adoo* surrenders, further reducing the PFLOAG numbers and support exponentially. Or, as Major General Jeapes emphasized, killing an *adoo* reduced PFLOAG numbers by one. Encouraging an *adoo* to surrender reduced PFLOAG numbers by one and increased *firqat* numbers by the same amount, in addition to the increased support to the Sultan by the tribal members when their sons safely returned home.[246] The information service exploited this. The establishment of a communications strategy to exploit these events is an example of the convergent nature of conflict.

The information service exploited physical actions by emphasizing successful military operations and the creation of wells, while minimalizing *adoo* success and other unfortunate events as minor set backs. They also protected the campaign by building a communications infrastructure that allowed for quickly informing the Dhofaris, Omanis,

---

[246]Jeapes, 39; CF20110914W0001, interview; author's assessment.

and the Arab community of events, denying PFLOAG the opportunity to manipulate the information.[247] The convergence of the physical, informational, and cognitive dimensions were evidenced throughout the campaign.

The information service was able to execute an effective communications strategy because of the small size of the operation, central control of the greater campaign under the Sultan's direct leadership, and the personal initiative of its members. The significance of the information service is that it was executing the functions of information operations before the concept had been created by either the United States or British militaries. Its integration into the overall counterinsurgency campaign contributed to the success of the British military in Dhofar, and will become a point of comparison with the United States in Iraq in the following chapters of this thesis.

---

[247]Such as the aircraft accidents mentioned previously.

CHAPTER 5

THE 1st INFANTRY DIVISION IN SOUTHERN IRAQ

The 1st Infantry Division (1ID) was an US Army command that executed an IO centric campaign strategy during its deployment to southern Iraq, 2010 to 2011.[248] The actions of the 1st Infantry Division demonstrates how information operations were integrated into US Army operations.

Although not specifically referenced during planning, the principles of the previously reviewed military theorists were evident within the campaign strategy. Galula emphasized adaptability, and along with the Thompson, Kitson, and McCuen, firmly supported the use of propaganda. All of the theorists recognized the role that information played within a conflict, and suggested that government forces use information via propaganda to neutralize adversarial influence, secure popular support, and legitimize the government while emphasizing the unlawfulness of adversarial groups.[249]

The 1st infantry Division planners integrated IO into operations from the onset of campaign planning, which was evidenced by the division's staff structure and the campaign strategy's lines of effort. The role of information was emphasized within all operations as the division attempted to create a synergized effect through the convergence of public affairs, civil affairs, and offensive IO activities, and the use of civil capacity as

---

[248]The author was a member of the 1st Infantry Division during its tour to Iraq, and recognizes that his personal ties to the division put's the validity of this thesis at risk. The purpose of this chapter is not to present a biased critique of the performance of the 1st Infantry Division nor present a 'this is how we won the war' story. The actions and operations of the 1st Infantry Division as they pertain to IO will be critically examined and offered solely as examples of how IO may be integrated into military operations.

[249]Previously reviewed in Chapter 2, "Military Theorist Review."

a way to support Department of State public diplomacy efforts. Finally, offensive IO was used as a 'cognitive weapon system'. The Special Programs section and the division's use of public information actively sought to discredit adversarial actions while emphasizing the primacy of the Government of Iraq and the professionalism of the Iraqi Security Forces.[250]

The operating environment and threat

Iraq's southern nine provinces comprised the 1ID area of responsibility (AOR), operationally identified as United States Division-South (USD-S). The AOR was formed when the 10th Mountain Division, then responsible for Multi-National Division-South, merged AORs with the British forces in Multi-National Division-South East (Basrah). Babil, Najaf and Karbala, located close to Baghdad, were religious centers of influence. Dhi Qar and Diwaniyah (formerly called Qadisiyah) straddled the Tigris-Euphrates river valley, and Muthanna, the most impoverished of the nine, was to the south west along the Kuwaiti border. Wasit, also located next to Baghdad, and Maysan, a predominately marshy area, were located along the Iranian border. Basrah, the economic center for the USD-S, was located on both the Kuwaiti and Iranian borders, and was the location of Umm-Qasr Port, Iraq's only access to the Persian Gulf (see figure 4).[251]

---

[250]These activities will be examined in greater detail later in this chapter.

[251]Ralph Kauzlarich, interview by Darrell Vaughan, Fort Riley, KS, May 2, 2011.

Photo Removed Due to Copyright Restrictions

Figure 4.   Map of Iraq
Source: PBS Newshour, *Iraq*, http://www.pbs.org/newshour/indepth_coverage/
middle_east/iraq/map/map_flash.html (accessed November 23, 2011). This map depicts
the provinces, however the provincial names are dated. Babylon province is now Babil,
Qadisiyah is now Diwaniyah, and Thi-Qar is Dhiqar.

Threats within the USD-S AOR were SEGs and malign Iranian influence. The

southern provinces of Iraq were predominately Shia, a denomination of the Muslim faith.

Sunnis, the religious majority of the Muslim faith (except in Iraq) and rivals to the Shia,

had dominated political and government leadership positions during the Saddam Regime.

Saddam suppressed the southern Shia population for four decades, leaving southern Iraq

impoverished and the populace persecuted and "denied participation in government decisions."[252] With the removal of the Saddam regime, Shia clerical leadership strove to establish themselves in the Iraqi political establishment. Three groups emerged, the Asaib Ahl al-Haqq (AAH), the Katha'ib Hezbollah (KH), and the Sadrists, all supported with funding, training, and equipment by Iran.[253]

Muqtada al-Sadr, the son of assassinated cleric Mohammed Sadeq al-Sadr, led the Shia uprising of 2004.[254] He formed the Mahdi Army (the Jaysh al-Mahdi, or JAM), based in Sadr City, Baghdad, and conducted attacks against US forces, with the purpose of forcing American forces to leave Iraq. Sadr expanded his influence in Southern Iraq and was able to seize control of Basrah from the British forces. The JAM were allowed to enforce their own laws on the local populaces, which resulted in atrocities such as rapes and murders against 'improperly' dressed women.[255] Also, the JAM used intimidation to force the Iraqi Security Forces (ISF) and Iraqi local government leadership to not target high value JAM members.[256]

---

[252]Randal A. Dragon, interview by Ken Crowe, Basra, Iraq, December 26, 2010.

[253]Bill Roggio, "The Long War Journal: Iranian-backed Shia terror group remains a threat in Iraq: General Odierno," *The Long War Journal* (July 13, 2010), www.longwarjournal.org/archives/2010/07/iranianbacked_shia_t_1.php (accessed October 6, 2011).

[254]Baathists killed Mohammed Sadeq al-Sadr, a Shiite cleric who openly defied Saddam Hussein, in 1999. His son, Muqtada al-Sadr, based his legitimacy on his father's popularity.

[255]Alexander Alderson, "The Validity of British Army Counterinsurgency Doctrine after the War in Iraq 2003-2009" (PhD Thesis, Cranfield University, 2010), 164.

[256]3d Brigade Combat Team, 4th Infantry Division, "Transfer of Authority Brief to LTG Cone and CSM Cole and Belfieldman," May 13, 2010.

The British forces based in Basrah planned and executed operation Charge of the Knights with the ISF in March 2008.[257] The operation ended with the Sadrists' power base severely disrupted.[258] Yet, despite their reduction in influence over the southern Iraqi population, the Sadrists, led by Muqtada al-Sadr in Iran, would be the primary adversary of the 1ID. The JAM would later be re-named the Promised Day Brigade (PDB), a smaller militia consisting of vetted former JAM members, supported by Iran, tasked with disrupting security operations and destabilizing the nationalization process.[259]

The AAH originated as part of the Sadrist movement. Led by Qais Khazali, a former student of Mohammed Sadeq al-Sadr, the AAH separated from the Sadrists in 2004 due to differences of strategy with the Sadrists. The AAH emerged as an organization in 2006, organized similar to the Lebanese Hezbollah model[260] and supported by Iran's Islamic Revolutionary Guard Corps-Qods Force (IRGC-QF).[261] They conducted attacks against US Forces until late 2009, when the AAH leadership sought re-conciliation with the Government of Iraq. The organization was placed on the United

---

[257]Carter Malkasian, "Counterinsurgency in Iraq: May 2003-January 2010," in *Counterinsurgency in Modern Warfare*, ed Daniel Marston and Carter Malkasian (Oxford: Osprey Publishing, 2010), 306.

[258]Prior to this time, Muqtada al-Sadr had traveled to Qom, Iran, to begin his ayatollah clerical training, yet reportedly continued to direct JAM activities.

[259]Bill Roggio. "The Long War Journal: Iranian-backed Shia terror group remains a threat in Iraq: General Odierno."

[260]The Lebanese model extends influence by providing essential services to neglected population centers in exchange for fighters to conduct operations against an adversary.

[261]Marissa Cochrane, "Asaib Ahl al-Haq and the Khazali Special Groups Network," *Institute for the Study of War,* January 13, 2008, www.understandingwar.org (accessed October 6, 2011). The IRGC-QF, also referred to as the IRGC or Qods Force, is Iran's elite Special Operations branch.

States Forces-Iraq no target list at that time, which restricted operations against the AAH. Because of this, the AAH's activities were minimal during the 1ID tour in USD-S.

The Kata'ib Hezbollah, similar to the AAH, emerged in southern Iraq in 2006 in the vacuum left from the disruption of the Mahdi Army. The KH formed to conduct attacks against the US and other interventionist powers with the purpose of ending foreign intervention in Iraq and establishing a Shiite Islamic government. The Qods Force used the KH, along with other SEGs, as a means for extending Iranian influence in Iraq by assisting with the arming and training of KH operatives. The KH operated primarily in and around Baghdad and in Wasit, Maysan, and Najaf provinces.[262]

Common to all of the SEGs operating in southern Iraq was support from Iran. Working through a combination of front companies and the SEGs, Iran sought to increase Iraqi dependence on Iranian services. Iranian products were available at lower prices than similar Iraqi products, electricity was provided by Iranian power plants to southern Iraq, and Iranian front companies, such as hotels, controlled the religious tourism of Najaf and Karbala. Maysan province, located along the Iranian border, became an operational support zone for Iranian supported SEGs, specifically the KH.[263] Iran became a competitor of the United States, each country vying for positioning as a preferred partner of the Government of Iraq.[264]

---

[262]Informatics Team at the International Centre for Political Violence and Terrorism Research, "Kata'ib Hezbollah," *Political Violence and Terrorism Research* (March 5, 2010), 2 and 5, www.pvtr.org/pdf/GroupProfiles/Kata'ibHezbollah-05March10.pdf (accessed October 6, 2011).

[263]3rd Brigade Combat Team, 4th Infantry Division Transfer of Authority brief.

[264]Kauzlarich interview; Charles Loi, *U.S. and Iranian Strategic Competition: Competition between the US and Iran in Iraq* (Washington, DC: Center for Strategic and

The 10th Mountain Division assumed responsibility for USD-S in May 2009, and

transitioned responsibility to the 36th Infantry Division in September of the same year.

Basrah International Airport, located to the north west of the city of Basrah, became the

location of the division headquarters. The 1st Infantry Division relieved the 36th Infantry

Division in late January 2010.[265]

Operational challenges

The 1st Infantry Division had several operational challenges once they assumed

responsibility for their AOR. This was seen through the expansion of operational

responsibility, the challenges of the Iraqi political climate, the operational transition from

Operation Iraqi Freedom to Operation New Dawn, and the persistent malign Iranian

influence.

There was the expansion of operational responsibility while executing the United

States Forces-Iraq's 'Reduction of Forces' strategy. The AOR, which had been divided

between US and British forces, consolidated while USD-S reduced from four maneuver

brigades to two.[266] Associated with Reduction of Forces was the movement of equipment

and materiel through the USD-S sector. Large convoys were potential targets of the Shia

International Studies, March 2, 2011), www.csis.org/Burke/studies (accessed November 20, 2011).

[265]Kauzlarich, interview.

[266]Jefforey Smith, interview by Louie Cheng, Iraq, May 15, 2009.

Extremist Groups (SEGs), who continued to conduct rocket, sniper, and improvised explosive device attacks against USD-S forces.[267]

The Iraqi political climate was difficult to work within. Counter to the theorists' shared principle of the requirement for both the primacy of the government and all actions unified under a single command or leader, the Government of Iraq was a fractious body that did not form after the Iraqi national elections held in March, 2010. Prime Minister Maliki remained as the interim prime minister, whereas the Iraqi governing body was a fractured organization with varying agendas, often influenced by Iranian involvement. The southern Iraq provincial leadership was selected by Maliki, and could be removed at his request. The result was a large, beureaucratic organization often working at odds with itself. The provincial leadership were not included as part of the military chain of command nor given approval authority of military operations. However, they were often consulted prior to operations. The three regional operation centers facillitated this cooperation and partnership.[268]

The transition from Operation Iraqi Freedom to Operation New Dawn was projected to occur in September 2010, and symbolized the overall transition from

---

[267]CB20110906P0001, interview by Darrell Vaughan, Fort Leavenworth, KS, August 6, 2011. Attacks continued to happen throughout the length of 1ID's tour, although not at the same volume as USD-C and USD-N. The 1ID suffered one KIA during its tour.

[268]CB20110906P0001, interview. The three coordinating centers were the Basra Operating Center in the south, the Mid-Euphrates Operating Center to the north near Baghdad, and the Maysan Operating Center to the northeast in Maysan province. These were referred to by their acronyms: the BaOC, MEOC, and MaOC respectively. The operating centers were in command of all forces, provided a single point of control for security operations and allowed for the integration of political leaders into security operations.

offensive operations to stability operations within greater Iraq. The operational effect was the cessation of uni-lateral US military operations. The units under USD-S's command would only be allowed to conduct partnered operations with the Iraqi Security Forces, and would transition fully into an advisory and assistance relationship.[269]

The security situation in southern Iraq was more stable than the other sectors, yet violence still occurred. Attacks were either bombings against the civilian population or IED and rocket attacks against US Forces. The security situation in November 2010 was not much different from that of January 2010, which allowed the criticism that the transition to Operation New Dawn was more timeline based than operationally determined. In preparation for the transition to Operation New Dawn, the 1ID leadership had organized the division to perform stability operations and to support the Brigade Combat Teams as they transformed into Advisory and Assistance Brigades.[270]

Balancing the malign influence of Iran focused the strategy of the 1ID. Iraq and Iran had a long, shared history, often violent, with one another. However, there were strong ties. Iran was predominantly Shia, as was southern Iraq, and many of the tribes in Wasit, Maysan, and Basrah provinces had familial ties spanning across the Iraqi-Iranian border. Muqtada al-Sadr was receiving his clergy training in Qom, Iran, and possibly the

---

[269]CB20110906P0001, interview; 3rd Brigade, 4th Infantry Division; author's analysis.

[270]Piscal interview; CB20110906P0001, interview; Richard Quire, interview by Darrell Vaughan, Fort Riley, KS, May 2, 2011; author's analysis. The 1ID command did monitor operational events, and used the operational environment to determine 1ID campaign focus changes.

most important tie when considering the presence of the US, Iranians were Middle

Eastern, whereas the US was not.[271]

Iran had strong economic ties with Iraq. Iranian goods were sold in Iraqi markets,

Iranian hotels provided lodging in the religious centers of Najaf, and Iran supplied

electrical power to Basra. Yet, Iranian goods and services were often sub-par, were priced

to undermine the Iraqi production or provision of similar goods and services, and created

an Iraqi dependence upon Iran. The 1ID's campaign strategy addressed countering

Iranian influence by developing the economy of southern Iraq, securing its borders, and

disrupting the efforts of violent extremist networks such as the PDB.[272]

Strategy and operations

The strategy was operationalized along four lines of effort (LOE): the continued

development of the ISF, civil capacity and essential services improvement, transition, and

communications.[273] The ISF LOE included operations with and the training of the Iraqi

Army, Iraqi Police, and the Border Police. The civil capacity LOE included the

completion of projects, improving essential services such as water and electricity, and

economic development. The transition LOE dealt with the turnover of USD-S

installations to the Government of Iraq and the planned withdrawal of US Forces from

Iraq. The communications LOE sought to synchronize the efforts of the other three LOEs

by informing target audiences of their successes, and, through offensive IO, disrupting

---

[271]CB20110906P0001, interview.

[272]CB20110906P0001, interview; Quire, interview; Piscal, interview; author's analysis.

[273]Dragon, interview; CB20110906P0001, interview; Kauzlarich, interview.

violent extremist networks. The division was organized prior to deployment to implement the lines of effort.[274]

The 1ID leadership determined that the proper integration of information operations into the overall campaign strategy would become key to success and organized the division staff to do so.[275] The staff structure was flattened and organized around three operational cells: Operations, Sustainment, and the Effects Coordination Cell.[276] Instead of having numerous staff elements reporting to the Chief of Staff, the number was reduced to three primary LOE staff leads, the G2, the G5, and the G6, which allowed the division to focus on effects based operations, warrant based operations, and sustainment operations.[277]

The G3 was assigned responsibility for the ISF LOE.[278] Members of the section, in addition to performing the traditional functions of a division Operations Section, planned and oversaw the training of the ISF and guided warrant based operations within the 1ID's AOR. The ISF cell was created ad hoc from available G3 personnel, who coordinated and synchronized the ISF advisory efforts of the subordinate brigades. The Fires Section, normally tasked with coordinating fire support for the division, was given

---

[274]CB20110906P0001, interview.

[275]CB20110906P0001, interview; Kauzlarich, interview.

[276]CB20110906P0001, interview; Kauzlarich, interview; Piscal, interview. The G7, G9, and PAO would informally be called the 'Gruesome Threesome' by the 1ID leadership and the G3 and DCoS-FX the Barons. The G4 did not have a moniker.

[277]Piscal, interview.

[278]The G3 is the doctrinal staff designation for both the staff section responsible for the day-to-day synchronization of division operations, and the title of the senior officer in charge of the staff element.

responsibility of warrant based targeting.[279] The G5-Plans section, usually a subordinate staff element within the G3, was kept separate, and reported directly to the division Chief of Staff, Colonel Piscal.[280] The Deputy Commanding General-Maneuver (DCG-M), Brigadier General Gibbs, provided LOE guidance and direction, and was the senior leader to conduct ISF relevant key leader engagements (KLE) with the ISF leadership.

The G4 was assigned responsibility for the Transition LOE.[281] The section conducted its traditional mission of sustainment operations while executing the LOE responsibilities of coordinating both the logistical flow of personnel, equipment, and materiel out of Iraq and the turnover of facilities to the Government of Iraq. The section included G4 personnel, the G8 (finance), the G1 (personnel), and the Division Surgeon. The G6-Signal section was kept separate from the Sustainment Cell. The Deputy Commanding General-Support, Brigadier General Dragon, was responsible for the Transition LOE and was the senior leader responsible for relevant KLEs with Iraqi provincial government leadership.[282]

---

[279]Warrant Based Targeting was the targeting of high value individuals with the purpose of facilitating arrests and prosecution within the Iraqi judicial system. In order for an individual to be approved for an arrest, sufficient evidence needed to be available in order to secure an arrest warrant from a provincial judge. Arrests were normally executed as part of bi-lateral operations, with the ISF as the lead.

[280]Piscal, interview; Kauzlarich, interview.

[281]The G4 is the doctrinal staff designation for both the staff section responsible for sustainment operations (normally logistics, medical, maintenance), and the title of the senior staff officer responsible for the section.

[282]Piscal, interview.

The Effects Coordination Cell was responsible for two LOEs, civil capacity and communications, with overall responsibility for assessing all four LOEs.[283] The cell, using the assigned officers of the G7-Information Operations section, was expanded beyond its normal authorizations. This expansion and the elevation of the position of the Deputy Chief of Staff-Effects was a departure from a normal doctrinal division staff organization. The position of the Effects Coordinator, usually a field artillery colonel in charge of the division Fires Section, was moved to and made responsible for the Effects Coordination Cell. The 1ID Commanding General recruited Colonel Ralph Kauzlarich, an infantry officer, to become the division Effects Coordinator. The position was elevated to Deputy Chief of Staff-Effects, so that he possessed the authority to lead the G7, G9, and PAO and provide guidance to other staff sections to better synchronize efforts within the four LOEs. Colonel Kauzlarich reported directly to the Division Chief of Staff while coordinating actions with the G3 and Transition Chief.[284]

An Information Operations Section is normally led by a lieutenant colonel, with two information operations majors and two PSYOP majors as the staff officers. The 1ID IO Section was the foundation the larger Effects Coordination Cell was built upon. The Public Affairs Office, the Civil Affairs Section, the Operations Research and Systems Analysis team (ORSA), and the Red Team, along with their related tactical enablers, were joined with the IO Section.[285] Other non-standard, AOR specific enablers, such as

---

[283]Kauzlarich, interview.

[284]Kauzlarich, interview; CB20110906P0001, interview.

[285]Kauzlarich, interview; Smith, interview; CB20110906P0001, interview; Department of Defense, Joint Publication 3-61, *Public Affairs* (Washington, DC: Government Printing Office, May 9, 2005), xi. Other tactical enablers included the

the Iraqi Assistance Task Force, the Human Terrain Analysis Team, the Engineer Assessment Team, and US Embassy and United States Forces-Iraq liaison officers were also assigned to the Effects Coordination Cell. The information operations section included the division PSYOP section, the KLE section, IO Targeting, IO Operations and Plans, and IO Special Programs. The Effects Coordination Cell had expanded from approximately eight members to over one hundred and fifty.[286]

The result of this expansion in duties and responsibilities allowed Colonel Kauzlarich to integrate effects based operations into both USF and Department of State operations across all of southern Iraq, and gave him the ability to "influence, persuade, or inspire selected audiences to do what we wanted them to do."[287] Colonel Kauzlarich, by being responsible for assessments through the ORSA, was given the ability to direct other

---

Mobile Public Affairs Detachment, the Civil Affairs Detachment, and the Tactical PSYOP Company. The placement of the PAO within the same section as the division PSYOP section is a point for criticism. The 10th Mountain Division kept the sections separated due to the potential perception of the loss of PAO credibility due to close association with PSYOP. Joint doctrine does not mandate a separation of the two, and gives the guidance that the PAO must be aware of PSYOP activities, but not participate in the planning or execution of PSYOP. The success of such an organization is both contextually and personality dependent.

[286]Kauzlarich, interview; CB20110906P0001, interview. The KLE section was responsible for synchronizing and assisting with preparing for the KLEs conducted by the 1ID leadership, (who were the lead engagers with the Iraqi leadership and populace). The IO Targeting Section was responsible for synchronizing targets with the Fires Section, IO Plans and Operations organized the day-to-day operations of the section and participated in long term planning efforts with the G5. The IO Special Programs Section was responsible for executing offensive IO.

[287]Kauzlarich, interview.

officers not within the Effects Coordination Cell. His influence cut across all LOEs, allowing him to direct and provide guidance to collect accurately and effectively.[288]

It was not a normal practice to have a separate Communications LOE as it was usually viewed as an activity that was present in the other three LOEs. The 1ID leadership determined that there was a need for a communications strategy that received direct guidance and approval from the Division Commander. Acting upon his guidance, the Effects Coordination Cell developed specific action plans in support of planned operations, synchronized themes and messages in support of the action plans, and tracked target audience actions in order to assess operations and revise the on-going strategy.[289]

The Communications LOE supported the other three LOEs through four objectives: countering violent extremists organizations, anti-corruption, good governance, and the ISF. The Effects Coordination Cell developed communications specific action plans to support these objectives, and were prioritized and integrated into the other three LOEs by operational phase. For example, at the beginning of 1ID's deployment, the Iraqi elections and formation of the government was the operational focus for the division. The communications strategy prioritized support to security operations, with the main effort of the communications plan focusing on the ISF and the elections, followed by countering violent extremist organizations, governance, then transition. The Division Commander reviewed the communications strategy every five weeks during the Communications LOE Board. Colonel Kauzlarich and the Effects Coordination Cell provided recommendations for changes in priority based upon operational assessments,

---

[288]Ibid.

[289]Kauzlarich, interview; CB20110906P0001, interview.

102

upcoming operations and population viewpoints and sentiments within the operating environment.[290] For example, 1ID talking points initially emphasized support to the Government of Iraq. However, feedback provided by the Iraqi Assistance Task Force indicated that the Iraqi populace had the perception that US Forces were not contributing to both security and civil capacity operations, and were not informed of US-Iraqi partnership efforts. The communications strategy was adjusted to include talking points of US contributions and other partnership efforts.[291]

The communications strategy integrated the information operations, civil affairs, and public affairs efforts in support of the other LOEs to amplify their effects.[292] Events were tracked by category, with effort placed in integrating more than one element. For example, the completion of a civil capacity project would be circulated in the news media and spread throughout the communities through PSYOP products and KLEs. Successful security operations, US-Iraqi partnership initiatives, and other significant events occurring with 1ID's AOR were also emphasized in this manner.[293]

---

[290]CB20110906P0001, interview.

[291]CB20110906P0001, interview. The PAO's activities included public information and command information programs, and used both the traditionally thought of information conduits, such as media releases, and more contemporary means, such as social media. The 1ID division used Facebook to provide both public and command information. Two profiles were created, one for audiences located at Fort Riley, and another for southern Iraq. The Fort Riley profile was accessible by any member of the division, and was used as a means to pass command information. The southern Iraq profile was used to emphasize successful Iraqi-US partnership efforts, such as security and civil capacity operations.

[292]Kauzlarich, interview.

[293]CB20110906P0001, interview. The demonstrated both the relationship between security, civil capacity, and the information environment and the convergent nature of conflict.

The integration of the three pillars was demonstrated during the Communications Board to the commanding general. The Effects Coordination Cell graphically demonstrated the integration of messages by displaying the three pillars and the number of events that were singularly, doubly, and thrice exploited by the three pillars. For example, the completion of a civil capacity project with no accompanying media release was depicted as a 'one'. The completion of a project with an accompanying media release from the PAO was a 'two', and the completion of a project with both a media release and a PSYOP message emphasizing the legitimacy of the Government of Iraq was a 'three'. The number of 'three' operations provided an indication of the degree of integration of the three pillars.

The Effects Coordination Cell synchronized operations both internally and with the subordinate brigades in a weekly communications working group which focused upon upcoming events and operations.[294] For example, the Effects Coordination Cell developed talking points that supported the Rule of Law, the democratic process, and the legitimacy of the Government of Iraq, which were used before, during, and after the Iraqi national elections. Special Programs used offensive IO messages emphasizing ISF professionalism and their capability to provide security. The brigades conducted KLEs with influential provincial leaders using those talking points, which were synchronized during the communications working group, which emphasized the professionalism of the ISF and encouraged the Iraqi populace to participate in the elections. As a result, despite SEG intimidation and attacks, the 1ID contributed to over 52 percent of the southern Iraqi

---

[294]CB20110906P0001, interview; 3rd Brigade Combat Team, 4th Infantry Division, "Leader's Talking Points Staff Product," April 18, 2010.

population voting in the elections.[295] The Effects Coordination Cell exploited adversarial attacks during the elections.

The IO Special Programs section used offensive IO to counter the influence of violent extremist networks in USD-S.[296] Special Programs' tasks were to disrupt and delegitimize SEGs and other VENs while supporting the Government of Iraq, the democratic process, and the Rule of Law. Shia extremist groups often used disaffected former JAM members to conduct attacks against both US forces and Iraqi citizens. Special Programs emphasized the 'criminal' actions of the attackers, and attributed blame of Iraqi deaths and damage to civilian or Iraqi government property and facilities to the SEGs.[297]

For example, an ISF soldier, while protecting civilians at a polling station, was killed by an improvised explosive device. In August of the same year, a series of explosions in the Basrah market caused in excess of one hundred civilian casualties. The results of these unfortunate attacks allowed USD-S to further delegitimize SEGs through a variety of means, labeling the 'PDB freedom fighters' as 'criminals' instead. These attacks continued to work counter to the aims of SEG leadership. In October 2011,

---

[295]James B. Champagne, interview by Ken Crowe, Basra, Iraq, December 23, 2010.

[296]Security classifications prevent an in depth discussion of the capabilities used and operations executed by Special Programs. Use of common doctrinal terms does not violate OPSEC. Discussion of specific deception operations is not permitted.

[297]Quire, interview; CB20110906P0001, interview. Special Programs was originally composed of three majors, one each PSYOP, IO and Space functional area specialties, and one military intelligence non-commissioned officer. The Space functional area is a specialized staff function that is involved with satellite imagery, communications, and other special technical capabilities.

Muqtada al-Sadr would make public announcements to his followers in Iraq to cease attacks on US Forces because of the perception of instability the attacks created, which could have possibly created the grounds for US Forces to remain in Iraq past the December 2011 deadline.[298]

The PDB was the primary adversarial target group for Special Programs. A "gentlemen's agreement" was established dividing the responsibilities of targeting and conducting operations against AAH and KH amongst other organizations and entities operating within USD-S's AOR.[299] This allowed the various organizations and the 1ID to conserve resources by focusing on single target sets instead of broadly applying their efforts against multiple targets spread across southern Iraq.

Special Programs' integration with both division staff elements and the brigades was not always successful. Only one of the two brigades regularly used the capabilities of the Special Programs section. This was due in part to the proximity of the one brigade to the division headquarters (the brigade S7 was located on FOB Basrah), the result of a self-identified poor job of salesmanship on behalf of the Special Programs officers, the operational requirement for limited knowledge of activities, and that the brigade S7s were overtaxed with other responsibilities. This challenge to integration also existed within the division staff. For example, the Special Programs cell was not integrated well with

---

[298] Raheem Salman, "Iraqi cleric calls halt to attacks on US troops," *Los Angeles Times*, http://articles.latimes.com/2011/sep/12/world/la-fg-iraq-sadr-20110912 (accessed November 23, 2011).

[299] CB20110906P0001, interview; Quire, interview. The "other" operations included other PSYOP, lethal action, and unilateral warrant based arrests against SEG targets. These types of activities were recommended by the military theorists reviewed in chapter 2.

warrant based targeting efforts, which resulted in missed opportunities to exploit the arrests of SEG members.[300] The al-Sharqi raid of February 12, 2010, provided an example of the lack of coordination amongst the division staff elements.

United States Forces conducted a raid to arrest members of the KH in the village of al-Sharqi. The raid resulted in civilian casualties and no arrests, and was conducted without the knowledge of the Effects Coordination Cell. SEG sympathetic members of the Maysan provincial government, who stated that the raid was a "massacre in every sense of the word," exploited the civilian casualties.[301] The Targeting Cell was aware of the raid, but did not coordinate with the Effects Coordination Cell due to OPSEC concerns. The Special Programs section was then tasked to develop the Consequence Management Action Plan, which integrated PAO, PSYOP, and KLEs by the brigades' and division's leadership, to mitigate the risks of another incident such as the al-Sharqi raid. Closer coordination between the Targeting Cell and Special Programs was established, which allowed for the sharing of sensitive information without compromising security. The Consequence Management Action Plan was integrated into

---

[300]Quire, interview; author's anlysis. It was a normal practice for members of the Special Programs section to offer assistance to the brigades in preparing operations. However, the brigades' unfamiliarity with the programs and their need to complete the requirements of their individual commanders pushed the use of Special Programs into the background of operations. The majority of Special Programs' operations were executed with the personal direction of the Division Commander, at times without the knowledge of the brigade commanders.

[301]Patrick O'Connor, "Iraq: US military raid on Iranian-backed terrorist organization," The Global Realm, http://theglobalrealm.com/2010/02/15/iraq-us-military-raid-on-%E2%80%9Ciranian-backed-terrorist-organisation%E2%80%9D/ (accessed November 23, 2011).

future operations, but synchronization between Special Programs and other staff elements remained a challenge.[302]

Special Programs was able to build effective partnerships with interagency and other military elements not assigned to the division but operating within the AOR, which resulted in a unity of effort of supporting operations.[303] They were able to synchronize operations with the other units by sharing information and assets, which allowed the amplification of the effects of programs normally kept separate from one another. This was done through a combination of special technical capabilities and the manipulation of information within the AOR.[304]

Civil capacity projects and public diplomacy

The division provided support to public diplomacy by supporting the Department of State and Provincial Reconstruction Team (PRT) operations.[305] Knowledge of civil-military projects completed by the PRT were amplified through the PAO and through PSYOP information conduits; each communicating synchronized themes and messages to their respective audiences with the purposes of strengthening US-Iraqi ties and countering the influence of Iran in southern Iraq.[306]

---

[302]CB20110906P0001, interview; Quire, interview; author's analysis.

[303]Ibid.

[304]Ibid. The author is unable to provide greater detail due to OPSEC.

[305]Kauzlarich, interview.

[306]CB20110906P0001, interview; Kauzlarich, interview. Civil capacity projects and the provision of essential services was a psychological tool used by the Government of Iraq, the 1ID, and Iran to gain support from the local populace. Colonel Kauzlarich stated, while discussing support to the Department of State, that the completion of a

The communications strategy in support of the Department of State placed US civilian leadership in the lead and emphasized Iraqi partnership with the PRTs.[307] Brigadier General Dragon explained that an emphasis was placed on the US civilian leadership to support the transition from military to civilian led operations. He continued by explaining that the shift in focus did not mean that military was leaving, but rather the nature of the relationship was changing in order to prepare for a long term US strategic partnership with Iraq.[308] The strategy included informing audiences of completed, high profile projects that were potential US failures and "monuments of incompletion."[309] Public information and key leader engagements conducted by the division's leadership with the Iraqi leadership promoted economic development by focusing on agribusiness and sustainable essential services while emphasizing that security was tied to international investment.[310]

'friendly action' was used to garner support from "friendly audiences" while at the same time figuratively "poking the Iranians in the eye" by emphasizing uncompleted and substandard Iranian projects. For example, during a drought period, Iran provided a large amount of water to Basra, which was found to be non-potable. The event was exploited by emphasizing that Iran gave Iraq water that could not be used.

[307]Dragon, interview.

[308]Ibid. The military was not leaving at that time. Two years later, in December 2011, all US military forces would leave Iraq in compliance with the security agreement.

[309]Kauzlarich, interview.

[310]3rd Brigade Combat Team, 4th Infantry Division, "Leader's Talking Points Staff Product"; Dragon, interview. Emphasizing that stability and security would enable greater economic opportunities for Iraqis became a common USD-S talking point. For example, Southern Iraq, has numerous archeological and religious sites and is a popular destination for religious tourism. The holy cities of Najaf and Karbala have influenced over four hundred million Shia worldwide, and Najaf was named the Islamic Center of Culture for 2012.

Interagency cooperation was vital in Iraq. The Department of State presence in southern Iraq was a small organization with a limited presence in theater, whereas the 1ID was a large organization with many resources. The Division Commander prioritized support to the Department of State and ensured that support from the 1ID was available.[311] A result of the partnership efforts facilitated the establishment of the US Consulate in Basrah and developed a positive working relationship with the US embassy in Baghdad, the Office of Provincial Affairs, the Deputy Chief of Mission and the Assistant Chief of Mission for Transition.[312]

Civil capacity projects initiated by USD-S elements were integrated with economic development initiatives. The 1ID created the 'Economic Development Zone', based in Basrah province to stimulate small businesses and counter dependence on Iranian goods. The economic development plan focused on four areas: agriculture, support to international oil companies, small business development, and tourism.[313] Civil capacity and PRT programs provided agricultural support through the provision of monetary aid in excess of two hundred million dollars to farmers.[314] Civil capacity projects and initiatives were also used as a diplomatic means.

---

[311]CB20110906P0001, interview. Interagency cooperation is an area critiqued by the 1ID leadership. Even though the efforts were made to support the Department of State, events did not always go as planned, and this was identified as an area of improvement for the division. Sharing of information between 1ID and the PRTs was difficult at times.

[312]Dragon, interview. These offices were United States officials of the Department of State operating in Iraq.

[313]Ibid.

[314]Reginald E. Allen, interview by Matthew J. McDermit, Iraq, June 20, 2011.

The division used civil capacity projects, such as assisting with the construction of the Basrah Children's Hospital, to continuously improve the relationship between the United States with Iraq. The Basrah Children's Hospital was a project that had suffered numerous setbacks; which resulted in delaying its opening and creating the perception that the United States could not meet its promises and commitments. The division worked to connect power, water and sewage to the facility, and assisted with locating the facility's oncology equipment that was being held in Umm Qasr Port. In preparation for the facility's opening in September 2010, the division aided the hospital and provincial leadership by developing a phased plan for the delivery of services and in identifying what oncology equipment was needed. The opening of the hospital was viewed as a success in strengthening Iraqi and US relations by the 1ID leadership.[315]

Diplomatic efforts from the division's leadership aided in establishing a long-term relationship between Iraq and Department of State planners, and set the conditions for the Basrah Consulate build-out.[316] The military was in support of the Department of State, but it took time for members of the 1ID to realize that fact, which did have an affect on the 1ID's relationship with the Department of State. The PRTs were not synchronized with USD-S, and at times refused to share information or coordinate efforts with the civil affairs cell.[317] However, the relationship between the members of the Department of State and the 1ID weren't completely soured. Efforts to publicly place the Department of State

---

[315]Ibid.

[316]Ibid. The need to have a better understanding of the interagency process was identified as an area of improvement by COL Piscal.

[317]CB20110906P0001, interview.

111

in the lead of operations helped strengthen both the Department of State's relationship with USD-S and with the Iraqis.[318]

Operations security

Responsibility for OPSEC belonged to the Protection Cell of the 1ID division staff. Although the Effects Coordination Cell did not have responsibility for division OPSEC and did not regularly plan OPSEC measures into operations, the division was able to achieve an effective level of information security during the deployment. There were two instances of effective OPSEC, both a result of the careful control of information within the AOR. The first occurred after a USF base had been closed. Two days after the facility had been turned-over to Government of Iraq officials, SEGs conducted a rocket attack on the location, effectively attacking an empty sand barrier. The transition had intentionally been conducted maintaining a low profile, resulting in local SEGs being unaware that the facility had been closed.[319] The second was the movement of a Stryker Brigade Combat Team through the USD-S AOR. Attention was intentionally drawn, via media releases, to the completion date of the move, avoiding mention of movement routes and time tables. The operation was concluded two weeks ahead of schedule, resulting in no attacks on any movement convoy.[320]

How the 1ID executed OPSEC brings to focus whether or not an operation is an information related activity. The routine adherence to OPSEC measures is not necessarily

---

[318]Dragon, interview.

[319]CB20110906P0001, interview.

[320]Ibid.

considered information related activities. The deliberate control of information, such as not overemphasizing the base closures and the drawing of attention away from the movement of units through the 1ID AOR, which were deliberately planned into 1ID operations, are information related activities.[321]

The Southern Iraq Assessment Model

The ORSA element developed the Southern Iraq Assessment Model (SIAM) to allow assessment of USD-S operations. The ORSA element developed measures of effectiveness and measures of performance for each LOE, and applied the measures to each province individually. The LOE chiefs converted quantitative and qualitative measures into statistical values to show SIAM trends within the provinces.[322]

A criticism of any assessment model is that the unit in question begins at the low end of the spectrum and gradually demonstrates progress throughout its deployment, resulting in a much higher success rating at the end of their tour. The SIAM showed trends, but any changes had to be justified by the LOE chiefs. It was an honest broker approach to assessments that encouraged the LOE chiefs to honestly report trends. Major General Brooks did not force his staff to show continuously improving statistics. If a province showed a decline in a particular measure of effectiveness, Major General Brooks would ask for the justification, and elicit discussion on how to respond. The

---

[321]Author's analysis.

[322]CB20110906P0001, interview; Kauzlarich, interview; Quire, interview.

SIAM showed a slight improvement in the majority of the provinces, and a decline in others, at the completion of 1ID's tour.[323]

The challenge of assessments was evident with the Special Programs section. Qualitative collection was done through operational reports, intelligence collection, open source intelligence collection, HTAT and IQATF reports, public perception data, and a variety of other collection means. Events had to be looked at "with an honest eye in order to determine whether or not it was a Special Programs initiative that had had an effect."[324] Sometimes, the feedback was concrete, but most times, not. Measuring the effects of influence operations is a challenge. The SIAM approach was an innovative attempt to link events occurring within the operational environment to a trend analysis that permitted Major General Brooks to provide guidance to his LOE chiefs.[325]

Conclusion

The military theorists emphasized the role of information and its application to operations within a conflict. Three analytical constructs, based upon the principles of Kitson, Thompson, McCuen, Galula, and Hoffman, were provided to analyze the relationship of the information environment to government forces, the operations they conduct against adversaries, and the general nature of conflict itself. The activities of the 1ID in southern Iraq provided opportunities to examine the application of those constructs to US Army operations.

---

[323]CB20110906P0001, interview; Quire, interview.

[324]Ibid.

[325]CB20110906P0001, interview; author's analysis.

The manner in which IO was integrated into the 1ID campaign strategy and executed within operations indicated adaptability. Galula espoused the organizing of government forces to address the context of the conflict in which it was involved; Kitson called this good coordinating machinery. The 1ID organized itself and designed its campaign strategy to meet the contextual requirements of its AOR. The 1ID campaign strategy was IO centric; the staff structure, LOEs, and the communications strategy were designed to integrated IO into all operations. This was evidenced by the elevation of the Effects Coordinator position to allow parity with the G3 and G4, the expansion of the Effects Coordination Cell, and the creation of a separate Communications LOE. Other indicators were the mental transition of thought from a military led campaign to the Department of State and the modification of plans and operations based upon assessments.[326]

The was frustration amongst the Effects Coordination Cell because of the perceived timidity and inactivity of their Department of State counterparts; as was indicated by the sometimes-difficult relationship between the 1ID civil affairs section and the PRTs.[327] The 1ID leadership made the conscious effort to visibly place the Department of State in the lead and use civil capacity projects as a way of supporting public diplomacy. The communications strategy emphasized the accomplishments of the

---

[326]Kauzlarich, interview; CB20110906P0001, interview; author's analysis. Civilian primacy in leadership is a key point within the writings of classic counterinsurgency theorist Galula.

[327]Ibid.

civilian leadership and provided division assets to the Department of State elements in order to aid in their mission.[328]

Special Programs did not fully integrate its capabilities until six months into the deployment, and the Effects Coordination Cell was initially reactionary in response to events within the AOR. Efforts were made by the Effects Coordination cell to become less reactionary, such as the development of the Consequence Management Action Plan, and strengthened relations with subordinate units, interagency entities, and other military elements operating with in the USD-S AOR.[329]

The division reorganized its maneuver units and modified their missions to meet the demands of the operating environment and changes in mission throughout the length of its deployment. The division expanded brigade operational responsibilities as US Forces continued to draw down.[330] Under Operation New Dawn, the brigades transitioned from having the authority to conduct unilateral security operations to a bilateral advisory mission.[331] The communications strategy changed to include informing the Iraqi populace of the contributions made by US Forces. The 1ID continued to demonstrate adaptability, facilitated by the ORSA SIAM, and guided by the commanding general, throughout its deployment.[332]

---

[328]Dragon, interview; author's analysis.

[329]CB20110906P0001, interview; Quire, interview; author's analysis.

[330]Author's analysis.

[331]Champagne, interview; author's analysis. This transition was difficult for some members of the brigade combat teams, who wanted to continue executing operations as they had during previous deployments.

[332]CB20110906P0001, interview; author's analysis.

The interrelated nature of security, civil capacity, and the information environment was demonstrated by the 1ID's efforts to promote public diplomacy through civil capacity projects and partnered security operations. The 1ID deployed into a theater that was, relatively speaking, secure, and determined that the division had made the transition from offensive operations to stability operations.[333] Civil capacity projects, both new and previously existing, continued to be executed by both the division and the PRTs. With the transition from Operation Iraqi Freedom to Operation New Dawn, the division realized that funding and resources would become scarcer and sought to complete ongoing projects. The completion of projects was advertised to the Iraqi populace, emphasizing the role of the Department of State and the Iraqi provincial leadership in order to support the primacy of civilian leadership and aid public diplomacy.[334]

The completion of civil capacity projects, and the amplification of their success, would not have been possible or believable without the relative security that existed in southern Iraq. The ISF and US Forces continued to conduct bilateral operations, which were exploited through the communication strategy to strengthen US-Iraqi ties. Attacks did occur, however, they were used to further delegitimize the actions of SEGs. The exploiting of civil capacity successes and improved security conditions demonstrated the interrelated nature of civil capacity, security, and the information environment.[335]

---

[333]Dragon, interview; Kauzlarich, interview; Piscal, interview; author's analysis..

[334]Piscal, interview; Kauzlarich, interview; CB20110906P0001, interview; author's analysis.

[335]Kauzlarich, interview; CB20110906P0001, interview; author's analysis.

117

The integration of the three pillars of effects (PAO, CA, and IO) within the communications strategy provided an example of the convergent nature of conflict. The Iraqi media, USD-S, and the SEGs quickly acted upon physical actions, such as arrest raids or the completion of civil capacity projects. Knowledge of events was transmitted through a variety of information conduits, such as over telecommunications networks, Internet chat rooms, and traditional news media outlets. Actors within the operating environment sought to manipulate information to meet their individual agendas. Shia extremist group leadership often attempted to delegitimize the efforts of USD-S and the Government of Iraq, whereas the 1ID attempted to bolster the Iraqi government and the ISF.[336]

To claim a successful tour for the 1ID is not the purpose of this case study and would be a fallacy similar to those of other works provided by authors writing about their units' tours in theater. The 1ID was successful in some regards as well as unsuccessful in others, and success in Iraq remains to be determined. The activities of the 1ID does provide insight to the nature of conflict as examined through the analytical constructs provided in the Counterinsurgency Theorists Review chapter, and provides ways and means IO can be integrated into US Army operations.

---

[336]Kauzlarich, interview; CB20110906P0001, interview; Quire, interview; author's analysis.

CHAPTER 6

CONCLUSIONS AND RECOMMENDATIONS

The Dhofar and Iraq case studies provided evidence and examples of how IO may be integrated into military operations during periods of instability. However, the evidence does not suggest that there is a single method for integrating IO that is applicable to all types of conflict, instead providing suggestions of how to control and manipulate information within the context of the conflict in question. Dhofar and Iraq were very different from one another, and although the ways and means of integration were similar, IO at times supported differing objectives. Understanding the contextual differences of the two conflicts is necessary in order to understanding how to integrate IO into military operations.

Iraq and Dhofar: Contextual differences

Dhofar and southern Iraq, in terms of physical environment and culture, were very different, which affected the scale of the military operations conducted, the types of forces used, and the strategies that were implemented to fight the conflicts. Dhofar's environment required the use of both irregular and conventional military forces led by the British, whereas the 1ID was partnered with the Iraqi Army and Iraqi Police, who executed operations in southern Iraq within mostly urban areas.

Dhofar was a small, remote, undeveloped province, consisting of seasonally inhabitable highlands on the *jebel* and low coastal areas. The *jebel* was sparsely populated, inhabited by the migratory Dhofaris, who, despite being Islamic Arab tribesmen, were ethnically different from the remainder of Oman. Intra-state adversarial

119

influence and support was provided by the PDRY to the PFLOAG, a communist supported insurgent organization.[337]

Iraq was larger than Dhofar and more densely populated and urbanized. The majority of the population lived in dense population centers within the fertile areas between the Tigris and Euphrates Rivers, on the outskirts of Baghdad, and along the Iranian border. Desert dominated the southwestern portion of southern Iraq, mostly within the Muthanna province.[338]

Southern Iraq was dominated by the Shia denomination of Islam. Religion during the conflict was not a factor in the sense of whether or not the worship of Islam was persecuted. The Shia denomination did provide a cultural bond within southern Iraq communities, the cultural conduit for the anti-American rhetoric of the SEGs as well as a recruiting pool for VENs. Shia-sponsored violence was a result of the changing southern Iraq power structure as formerly suppressed Shia communities retaliated against former Sunni influence and oppression.[339]

Iran provided support to insurgent organizations in southern Iraq. One would think that, because Iranians are Persian and the history of conflict that exists between Iraq and Iran, that Iranian influence would be limited. However, familial ties, especially along the border, facilitated support and cross-border smuggling. Also, Iranians were both Shia

---

[337]Previously discussed in Chapter 4, Dhofar, 52-56.

[338]Previously discussed in Chapter 5, Iraq, 87-88.

[339]Previously discussed in Chapter 5, Iraq, 89-92.

and from the Middle East, whereas Americans were not, which provided a common enemy to both ethnic groups.[340]

The physical environments and cultural factors shaped how the British and Americans executed their military campaigns and affected the outcomes of their operations. Because of the Dhofar's relatively small area, the British were able to conduct their counterinsurgency campaign with approximately a brigade-sized element and a small number of enabler forces such as veterinarians. The British also had the support of the majority of the Dhofaris, especially as the PFLOAG increasingly lost support. The 1ID was responsible for a much larger area with a greater population, which required a division sized military force and numerous enabling forces and infrastructure. The 1ID did not have the full support of the population because of Shia cultural solidarity and Iranian influence.[341]

Contextual differences: Political climate

The communications strategies of both the British and the 1ID were affected by each conflict's political climates. Galula stated that the government, not the military, had primacy during periods of conflict.[342] The Dhofar campaign followed Galula's principle, whereas Iraq not as much. The leadership and political climates within both conflicts were different. Dhofar, was under the leadership of one person, Sultan Qaboos, whereas

---

[340]Previously discussed in Chapter 5, Iraq, 94-95.

[341]Previously discussed in Chapter 4, Dhofar, 57-79.

[342]Galula, *Pacificication in Algiers*, 244.

Iraq's government was a fractious bureaucracy led by an interim prime minister. This affected how IO messages were developed and approved within both conflicts.

Dhofar was led by a single individual, Sultan Qaboos, who was directly involved in the counterinsurgency campaign. All British military forces in Dhofar were in support of the Sultan's campaign plan and reported to the Sultan, not Britain. Sultan Qaboos's government approved all PSYOP messages, and provided guidance to the Dhofari Information Service as to what was said and how it was delivered.[343] The political climate of southern Iraq was not as unified, which caused the 1ID to not include the Iraqi leadership in its IO approval process.

A single leader did not lead southern Iraq. At the national level, Iraq's government did not form after the Iraqi National Elections because a single political bloc did not achieve the necessary votes required. Political maneuvering and deal brokering amongst the various political groups delayed the selection of the prime minister, the president, and the formation of the governing council and created political uncertainty within the provinces.[344]

The provincial leadership held their positions based upon the approval of Prime Minister Maliki and could be replaced easily. The 1ID leadership partnered with the provincial leadership, but did not report directly to them. Although the American campaign strategy was developed in partnership with and in support of the Government of Iraq, the strategy was designed to achieve American objectives. The 1ID was not subordinate to the Government of Iraq, and Iraqis were not involved in the approval of

---

[343]Previously discussed in Chapter 4, Dhofar, 64-67.

[344]Previously discussed in Chapter 5, Iraq, 93.

1ID messages, although Iraqi ex-patriots and local nationals were employed to aid in PSYOP product development. This brings to light the question of what degree the host nation government is to be involved in an interventionist power's operations within their country?[345]

In order to properly explore that question, the context of the conflict needs to be understood. Oman had a stable government led by a single individual. Iraq had an unstable government led by a prime minister who divided his attention between providing leadership to a much larger country with numerous power groups vying for political power, and personally maneuvering to protect his own position. Sultan Qaboos was personally involved with the running of the campaign, which facilitated British operations by providing a relatively streamlined chain of command and approval process. The 1ID leadership partnered with nine provincial leaders, each with a separate political agenda and possible ties to Iranian backed VENs. Prime Minister Maliki was not readily accessible by the 1ID leadership, and guidance from his office passed along US military channels. Approval of IO messages from the provincial leadership may have not been either possible or desired. The use of local leadership in operations is dependent upon the political stability of the conflict and the reliability of those local leaders invited to the planning process.[346] Host nation government involvement may not be desired by the interventionist power, and access to military operations should not be provided unless the host nation government is deemed reliable enough to actively participate. The Omani government was reliable, the provincial government of southern Iraq was not.

---

[345]Ibid.

[346]Author's analysis.

Adaptability

Galula stated that the government had the responsibility of understanding the context of the conflict, setting its campaign objectives, and organizing itself to win.[347] Adaptability is enabled by a thorough understanding of the conflict; its physical environment, culture, history, politics, the causes of the conflict and the adversaries. This thorough understanding of the conflict allows the military forces involved to develop strategies that allow them to be proactive with their operations, and effectively reactive when unforeseen events occur. Both the British and 1ID demonstrated their understanding of the conflicts in which they were involved.

The British assessed the Dhofari environment and developed the Watt's Plan to base its campaign plan upon. The Watt's Plan addressed the need for security, civil capacity projects, and a means for sharing the government's narrative. The SAS organized themselves into security training forces (the BATTS) and civil capacity delivering teams (the CATs). The Dhofari Information Service was created to provide propaganda support to BATT and CAT operations. Collectively, the British forces secured the Dhofari people and improved their quality of life by establishing wells, providing schools, and improving their economic opportunities.[348]

Although originally established to provide PSYOP support, the information service exercised initiative and increased its responsibilities to include involvement with all means of manipulating and controlling information within Dhofar. The Dhofari Information Service originally consisted of one individual, and expanded to include

---

[347]Galula, *Pacification in Algiers*, 244.

[348]Previously discussed in Chapter 4, Dhofar, 64.

Dhofari natives, eventually becoming the Ministry of Information. Operations were facilitated through personal relationships, demonstrated by the exchange of favors amongst the various other elements of the British military presence, such as providing aerial photography support to the air force. Opportunities within the environment were seized and acted upon, such as the use of the captured letter to create the official seal of the *adoo* leadership. The seal was subsequently used to insert disinformation into PFLOAG networks, resulting in the deaths of several adoo members.

The 1ID also demonstrated adaptability, the most prominent example being its IO centric staff organization. The Effects Coordination Cell contained offensive IO elements, the public affairs section, IO intelligence support sections such as the HTAT, the civil affairs section, and the division's organizational assessment team.[349] The 1ID was able to operate with its staff structure because of the Division Commander's understanding of IO and the personalities of the Effects Coordination Cell members.[350]

The 1ID, as with the Dhofari Information Service, also exploited violent adversarial actions by emphasizing the criminality of the attacks through a variety of information conduits. Government successes were emphasized, and opportunities to aid the Department of State were acted upon.[351]

---

[349]Smith, interview. There are commanders who choose to keep public affairs and the offensive IO sections, specifically the PSYOP elements, separated because of the perceived risk of compromising public affair's legitimacy. The 10th Mountain Division, during its tour in southern Iraq, separated the two for that reason.

[350]Previously discussed in Chapter 5, Iraq, 95-102.

[351]Previously discussed in Chapter 5, Iraq, 102-106.

For both the British and 1ID, a thorough understanding of the conflicts in which they were involved facilitated adaptability. When exploitable opportunities presented themselves, previous planning and preparation allowed for quick action on the part of both organizations' IO agencies. Their leadership fully understood the context of their conflicts and adapted their organizations to support their objectives. Success for the British has been demonstrated; Oman is now a wealthy, progressive member of the Arab community. Success for the 1ID has yet to be determined. However, the examination of the 1ID staff structure supports the re-organization of a unit to meet the requirements of the mission, provided the context of the conflict is taken into consideration.[352]

Security operations and the information environment

The terrain affected how security operations were conducted by both the BATTs and the 1ID. Dhofar's rugged, remote terrain required the use of British led regular and irregular forces. Security in southern Iraq, by comparison, was bi-lateral, provided by the ISF in partnership with US Forces and conducted within urban areas. Dhofar used British Special Forces whereas conventional military forces led Iraq. Both conflicts used indigenous people to provide security.[353]

Both the *firqat* irregular forces and the SAF provided security on the *jebel* by conducting attacks against *adoo* camps and through their armed presence within the tribal communities. The lack of a long-term Omani military presence on the *jebel* inhibited initial security efforts. The SAF conducted operations against the PFLOAG, however

---

[352] Author's analysis.

[353] Previously discussed in Chapter 4, Dhofar, 62, 79-80; Chapter 5, Iraq, 95-97.

because of both the rugged conditions and the substandard equipment they were equipped with in 1970, did not have the capacity to remain on the *jebel* and exploit their successes. The creation of the *firqat* forces allowed the Sultan to establish his authority with the Dhofaris, provide security and demonstrate his commitment through enduring civil capacity projects. Security operations were British led, in the case of the SAF, and BATT inspired when executed by the *firqat*. The *firqat* did not win the war for the Sultan, but their creation was a deciding factor in the overall success of the campaign.[354]

Violence in the 1ID sector, comparatively was less than within the other sectors of Iraq. Security operations were executed primarily as warrant based arrests instead of search and destroy operations, and conducted mostly within highly populated urban areas, such as Basra. The operations were bi-lateral, ISF led, and coordinated at the provincial level through the three regional operating centers. Violence was expressed as either bombings directed against civilian targets or rocket and IED attacks against US Forces. Security operations focused on the arrests of those individuals responsible for the attacks and the disruption of lethal aid networks.[355]

Security was provided in both campaigns. Improvement in Dhofar occurred after the formation of the *firqat*. Security was already established in Iraq, and the ISF enjoyed

---

[354]CF20110914W0001, interview; CF20110912J0001, interview; CF20110914DV0001, interview; previously discussed in Chapter 4, Dhofar, 62. The use of both irregular forces with knowledge of the jebel and familial ties to the *Jebalis* and conventional forces with the military capacity to destroy the *adoo* was a complimentary strategy. The *firqat* were difficult to lead. They would not operate outside of their tribal lands, and military operational objectives had to match tribal objectives before full cooperation could be expected. Blood feuds, and other tribal rivalries made multi-*firqat* operations tenuous.

[355]Kauzlarich, interview; Quire, interview; CB20110906P0001, Interview.

a high degree of confidence from the Iraqi people. Success in security operations were emphasized and exploited by the appropriate agencies in both conflicts, each supporting their respective government and delegitimizing adversarial activities within their respective AORs.

Civil capacity and the information environment

Civil capacity projects are an effective means for addressing the grievances of a disenfranchised population and demonstrating a government's commitment to improving the quality of life of its people. An interventionist power may assist with civil capacity projects as a way of establishing and strengthening diplomatic ties with the host nation government. Finally, civil capacity projects may be used as a form of population control by the removal of a provided service as a result of activities counter to the government's objectives being committed by the populace. The Dhofar and Iraq case studies provide evidence of each.

The CATs, acting in support of the Omani government's objectives, used civil capacity projects to demonstrate the commitment of Sultan Qaboos to the Dhofari people. Wells, roads, schools, medical, and veterinary support was provided to the *Jebalis*, but with the caveat that support to the Sultan was mandatory. Any discovered support to the *adoo* would result in the denial of the services. The establishment of wells created gathering places for the tribes, which would eventually become villages and towns. This facilitated crowd control by enabling the relatively easy assembly of people in an area, and the potential denial of services for *adoo* support ensured their compliance with the Omani government.[356]

The Department of State, a US civilian agency, had authority over civil capacity development in Iraq. The 1ID saw the civil capacity projects being executed within its AOR as an extension of defense support to public diplomacy. The division emphasized the transition to civilian leadership and the strengthened relationship between Iraqis and Americans during public engagements. Civil capacity projects were portrayed as the evidence that America was a partner to the Iraqis. In both case studies, improved economic and living conditions were the physical proof of their respective governments' best intents for their populations, which were exploited to generate support to their respective governments.[357]

The integration of information operations

Information operations transitioned from a technical concept created to disrupt an adversarial commander's communications network to a broader construct implementing any capability necessary to inform and influence target audiences within the an area of operations. The military theorists previously reviewed supported this action. Thompson specifically stated that a government had to control all of the information within a conflict, and Galula provided suggestions for how to use propaganda and PSYOP against adversaries.[358]

---

[356]Previously discussed in Chapter 4, Dhofar, 76-79.

[357]Previously discussed in Chapter 5, Iraq, 106-111.

[358]Previously discussed in Chapter 2, 11-22.

Confusion as to what IO was and hesitancy on how IO should be integrated stems from adherence to old paradigms, such as 'PSYOP is IO', and a commander's degree of confidence and comfort in its use. The introduction of the information engagement concept added to the confusion; US Army practitioners and commanders used IO as either another PSYOP-like capability or as a media engagement asset. Information operations practitioners became 'the media guys.' The emerging IO doctrine corrected these misperceptions by better stratifying IO capabilities, responsibilities, tasks and purposes.[359]

The name of IO was changed to better reflect the discipline's purpose; it is now called inform and influence activities. The doctrine provided in FM 3-13, *Information Operations*, implied IO ownership of capabilities by the use of the title 'core capabilities'; new doctrine specifically stated that IO does not own capabilities, that it is an integrating and coordinating staff function only.

The confusion between whether PSYOP, public affairs, or electronic warfare are the 'true form of IO' was resolved; US Army IO has three pillars: information related capabilities, IO planners, and intelligence support to IO. Information related capabilities were public affairs, PSYOP, electronic warfare, combat camera, and any other capability when used in support of, or integrated as, part of an IO activity within a larger unit's plan. The emerging doctrine acknowledged that these capabilities would be used in other capacities that are not IO related, such as the defensive nature of EW.[360]

---

[359]Previously discussed in Chapter 3, 43-47; author's analysis.

[360]Previously discussed in Chapter 3, 45; author's analysis.

Information operations planners were specialized staff members responsible for planning and integrating IO into mission orders. They are mostly the FA30 community, but can and will most likely include members from information related capabilities serving in a higher organization's planning cells. Intelligence support to IO included tactical support, HTATs, target audience analysis, and any other form of intelligence support that addresses the specific needs of IO planning. The usefulness of the intelligence clarification is that it aids in clarifying the purpose for the support within the intelligence community. A simple analogy for IO presented as a construction project is suggested as such: IO planners are general contractors, information-related capability providers are plumbers and carpenters, and intelligence support comes in the form of a hardware store clerk or an architect providing advice on a house design.[361]

The tasks of IO have come full circle; they are destroy, disrupt, degrade, deny, deceive, exploit, and influence. These tasks may be executed by any appropriate capability in a mission dependent capacity, ranging from (but not limited to) EW, to an infantry rifle company. The tasks of the short-lived information engagement era were inform and influence, which contributed to the confusion as to what IO's purpose was by focusing commander's and practitioners on the media and key leader engagements. The emerging doctrine corrected these misperceptions by removing IO from a media-centric focus and re-integrating the discipline as part of the larger US Army warfighting construct.[362]

---

[361]Ibid.

[362]Previously discussed in Chapter 3, 46-48.

The requirement to control information within a conflict was not a new revelation, much as the nature of war itself has not changed. Each of the military theorists reviewed in this thesis emphasized the need for controlling and manipulating information, expressed through the context of their time.[363] The context of conflict has changed though, and the doctrinal evolution of IO has occurred in response to those changes. The emerging doctrine attempted to clarify misperceptions and uncertainties as to how IO was to be integrated into military operations. This was simply a clarification, not new doctrine on how to implement IO.

The role of information was evident when examining both the relationship between security, civil capacity, and the information environment, and within the convergent nature of conflict. Information is a conceptual form of 'ammunition'; and information operations are the 'conceptual weapons' that connect physical events to cognitive affects through the control and manipulation of information. This activity is expressed through the four ways of integrating IO into military operations.[364]

The control of information leaving the area of operations informs friendly target audiences of events occurring within a conflict while protecting military operations. The act of controlling information sounds nefarious; it is not. The way in which information is controlled is context dependent, and is done through a variety of means such as through a commander's command information program, media releases to home and international

---

[363]Previously discussed in Chapter 2, 11-22.Normally expressed as PSYOP and propaganda, which is natural. The majority of the theorists based their principles upon mid-century conflicts; information operations were not introduced as a concept until 1976.

[364]Chapter 2, 23-27; author's analysis.

audiences, and the exercising of proper OPSEC measures. Full disclosure and transparency of operations may or may not be desired.

British support to Dhofar was provided with the caveat that the British people would have limited knowledge of its existence. Casualties were reported as training accidents. Sultan Qaboos maintained a pool of reporters on retainer to write stories favorable to the Omani government, and visitor movements were carefully controlled and executed so as to not endanger military operations and to provide the perception of progress and stability Sultan Qaboos wanted portrayed. Full disclosure of BATT deaths would have likely caused British popular support to Dhofar to cease, and the international media could have portrayed the Sultan's denial of wells to disloyal Jebalis as the sadistic actions of a monarch no better than his father.[365]

The 1ID in Iraq was not deceptive while controlling information leaving Iraq. The context of the conflict required accurate reporting, and it is illegal for the US Army to deliberately deceive US audiences. The 1ID used accurate media releases; unit sponsored social media, the commander's information program, controlled visitor movements, and selected talking points with both military and non-military dignitaries. That does not imply that full disclosure of 1ID operations occurred either. Proper OPSEC was prudently observed to protect sensitive operations, and talking points were relevant to visitors' agendas.[366]

The control of information within the area of operations focuses on neutral and friendly target audiences and applies to attributable messages that communicate the

[365]Previously discussed in Chapter 3, 63, 76-79.

[366]Previously discussed in Chapter 5, 69, 73.

government's narrative while delegitimizing adversarial activities. Both the British and 1ID conducted operations that promoted host nation government successes while protecting military operations and delegitimizing their adversaries. The use of propaganda and accurate and timely media releases providing the government's narrative are the means that readily to come to mind. The British exploited security successes and civil capacity gains through message boards, leaflet drops, and the news media. The government's narrative was truthful, a deliberate decision made by Sultan Qaboos in order to preserve the government's legitimacy. The 1ID exploited security and civil capacity gains through similar means, and also ensured that attributable-messages were truthful so as to preserve both the Government of Iraq's and US legitimacy.[367]

The manipulation of information was focused on adversarial target audiences and decision makers. This was accomplished through non-attributable information related capabilities and military deception. The British used deception to disrupt *adoo* networks by exploiting the inherent distrust and paranoia within PFLOAG, to discredit the PDRY with the United Nations, and to mislead the adoo as to what the Sultan's military capabilities were. The 1ID used integrated special technical capabilities and offensive IO to disrupt SEGs and VENs activities while emphasizing the criminality of their activities.[368]

Interwoven throughout all operations was the protection of information. The BATTs selectively released information pertaining to their operations in Dhofar to British audiences and visiting dignitaries. The 1ID either intentionally avoided emphasizing

---

[367]Previously discussed in Chapter 2, 65-75.

[368]Ibid.

certain operations, such as the movement of the maneuver brigade through their sector, or focused attention elsewhere. The routine activities of information protection, such as information assurance measures by the G6, or the proper handling of intelligence by the G2, are not inherently information related activities. Information related activities include the deliberate inclusion and omission of information as part of an overall strategy and plan.[369]

Recommendations

The conclusions above bring forth several recommendations. The first is that there is a need for commanders and planners to understand the context of the conflict in which they are involved. This goes beyond knowing the physical environment, the adversaries, and the reasons for the conflict. These factors not only affect the overall campaign strategy, but how IO is to be integrated into the strategy. How information is to be communicated, the means in which it is transmitted, and the intended audiences will be determined by the context of the conflict and will not be the same for other conflicts.

The second recommendation is for commander's to become more knowledgeable and comfortable with the use of IO. There are perceptions that IO is duplicitous by nature, which is not the case. There is also possible a sense of loss of control pertaining the manipulation of information. That is also not necessarily the case; careful planning and risk mitigation, as in any other operation, will reduce risks. Commanders should fully understand the tasks IO executes, and the relationship between information related capabilities, IO planners, and intelligence support. Through this understanding, they

---

[369]Previously discussed in Chapter 4, 65-75; Chapter 5, 111-112.

should become more comfortable with the integration of IO into their operations. That is not to say that if IO isn't integrated into an operation that it will fail. That is not the case, but the full effects of an operation will most likely not be realized.

Finally, there is a need to tear down old ways of thought in regards to IO. Debates as to what the function of IO is will continue until this is done. An IO focused search of the Combine Arms Library located at Fort Leavenworth, Kansas, will provide numerous masters thesis and monographs debating the purposes and functions of IO. Many of the documents take the position that Army IO is public information, or media, centric. The core capabilities discussed in those works are PSYOP, PA, and the efforts of IO are focused on information engagement. This is partly the fault of the IO Proponent Office of 2008, when the IE construct was introduced to its curriculum, and then further propagated within US Army conventional forces.[370]

Information operations, as was demonstrated by both the doctrinal review and the evidence provided by both case studies, is not a media-centric discipline. It is capable of much more, expressed in this thesis through the previously reviewed four ways of integration, provided the larger US Army community had a clearer understanding of IO tasks and structure. The emerging doctrine has clarified IO tasks and structure within a simple construct. Fully understanding the difference between information related capabilities and the overall IO doctrinal concept, and how the context of a conflict

---

[370]A typical IO qualification course class has forty-two students. The IE era lasted for approximately eighteen months, during that time, three to four classes teaching the IE focused curriculum were conducted, graduating approximately one hundred twenty FA30, IO practitioners. There are roughly two hundred and forty FA30s in the US Army, which implies that almost half of the IO practitioners for the US Army between 2008 and 2010 were influenced by the media-centric focus of the IE construct.

determines how the IO construct is to be integrated, should help in resolving any ambiguity.

Further research could be conducted on how IO is integrated into military operations during general war and stable peace. The application of IO during these two types of conflicts is potentially much different from how IO is integrated into unstable and insurgency conflicts.

Also, continued refinement of the emerging doctrine could provide better-clarified methods for IO integration, to include tactics, techniques, and procedures. Further discussion on this exceeds the scope of this thesis, however would aid in educating future leaders on IO.

BIBLIOGRAPHY

Primary Sources

Interviews

Command and General Staff College (CGSC) Scholars Program 2011. Scholars Program Counterinsurgency Research Study 2011. Research Study, Fort Leavenworth, KS: Ike Skelton Chair in Counterinsurgency, 2011. This study included interviews of counterinsurgency practitioners and policy professionals from the United States and United Kingdom. Each interview was executed as an oral history interview and adhered to Army policies of informed consent in compliance with federal law. Finally, each interview was coordinated through the Ike Skelton Chair in Counterinsurgency, CGSC Fort Leavenworth, KS.

Fort Leavenworth, KS

CB20110824M0001. A member of the Information Operations Propency Office. Interview by Darrell Vaughan. Fort Leavenworth, KS, August 24, 2011.

CB20110830W0001. A member of the Information Operations Propency Office. Interview by Darrell Vaughan. Fort Leavenworth, KS, August 30, 2011.

CB20110831H0001. A member of the Information Operations Propency Office. Interview by Darrell Vaughan. Fort Leavenworth, KS, August 31, 2011.

CB20110930H0002. A member of the Information Operations Propency Office. Interview by Darrell Vaughan. Fort Leavenworth, KS, September 30, 2011.

CB20110906P0001. A former member of the 1st Infantry Division Effects Coordination Cell. Interview by Darrell Vaughan. Fort Leavenworth, KS, September 6, 2011.

Fort Riley, KS

Kauzlarich, Ralph, Colonel. A former member of the 1st Infantry Division Effects Coordination Cell. Interview by Darrell Vaughan. Fort Riley, KS, May 2, 2011.

Quire, Richard, Major. A former member of the 1st Infantry Division Effects Coordination Cell. Interview by Darrell Vaughan. Fort Riley, KS, May 2, 2011.

Kmiecik, Liz, Major. A former member of the 1st Infantry Division Effects Coordination Cell. Interview by Darrell Vaughan. Fort Riley, KS, May 2, 2011.

Iraq

Allen, Reginald E. Interview by Matthew J. McDermitt. 3d ACR commander. Iraq, June 20, 2011.

Champagne, James B., Command Sergeant Major. The Division Command Sergenant Major, 1st Infantry Division. Interview by Ken Crowe. Basra, Iraq, December 23, 2010.

De La Paz, Enrique, Colonel. A former Red Team member. Interview by Ken Crowe. Basra, Iraq, December 10, 2010.

Dragon, Randal A., Brigadier General. The Deputy Commander-Support, 1st Infantry Division. Interview by Ken Crowe. Basra, Iraq, December 26, 2010.

Piscal, Richard, Colonel. Interview by Ken Crowe. Basra, Iraq, December 28, 2010.

Ronan, David W. A former member of the Human Terrain Team. Interview by Ken Crowe, Basra, Iraq, December 4, 2010.

Smith, Jefforey, Major General. Commander, 10th Mountain Division. Interview by Louie Cheng, Basra, Iraq, May 15, 2009.

United Kingdom

CF20110912J0001. A British Army Training Team commander. Interview by COIN Scholars Team 3. Warminster, England, September 12, 2011.

CF20110913C0001. A British Army Training Team commander. Interview by COIN Scholars Team 3. Warminster, England, September 13, 2011.

CF20110914DV0001. Former commanders and officers of the Sultan's Armed Forces and members of the British Army Training Team. Interview by COIN Scholars Team 3. Warminster, England, September 14, 2011.

CF20110914W0001. A former member of the Dhofari Information Service. Interview by Vaughan, Darrell. London, England, September 14, 2011.

CF20110917DV0001. Former commanders and officers of the Sultan's Armed Forces and members of the British Army Training Team. Interview by COIN Scholars Team 3. Warminster, England, September 17, 2011.

Official Reports, Memoranda, and Government Documents

3d Brigade Combat Team, 4th Infantry Division. "Transfer of Authority Brief to LTG Cone and CSM Coleman." Iraq, May 13, 2010.

————. "Leader's Talking Points Staff Product." Iraq, April 18, 2010.

British Military Source Files. *Dhofar Presentation* (United Kingdom: Date Unknown).

Chairman of the Joint Chiefs of Staff. Memorandum of Policy 30, version 1, *Command and Control Warfare.* Washington, DC: Government Printing, March 8, 1993.

Cochrane, Marissa. "Asaib Ahl al-Haq and the Khazali Special Groups Network." *Institute for the Study of War.* January 13, 2008. www.understandingwar.org (accessed October 6, 2011).

Department of Defense. Department of Defense Directive 3600.01, *Information Operations*, Draft. Washington, DC: Government Printing Office, 2011.

————. Department of Defense Directive 3222.4, *Electronic Warfare Administration.* Washington, DC: Government Printing Office, January 28, 1980.

————. Department of Defense Directive 3222.4, *Electronic Warfare (EW) and Command, Control, and Communications Countermeasures (C3CM).* Washington, DC: Government Printing Office, July 31, 1992.

————. Department of Defense Directive O-3600.1, *Information Operations.* Washington, DC: Government Printing Office, August 14, 2006.

————. Department of Defense Directive 4600.4, *Command, Control and Communications (C3) Countermeasures.* Washington, DC: Government Printing Office, August 27, 1979.

————. *Information Operations Roadmap.* Washington, DC: Governement Printing Office, October 30, 2003.

————. TRADOC Pamphlet (Pam) 525-69, *Military Operations Concept for Information Operations.* August 1, 1995. Information Warfare Site. http://iwar.org.uk/ iwar/resources/tradoc/p525-69.htm (accessed August 2, 2011).

Gates, Robert M. Memorandum for Secretaries of the Military Departments. *Strategic Communication and Information Operations in the DoD.* Washington, DC: Government Printing Office, January 25, 2011.

Informatics Team at the International Centre for Political Violence and Terrorism Research. "Kata'ib Hezbollah." *Political Violence and Terrorism Research.* March 5, 2010. www.pvtr.org/pdf/GroupProfiles/Kata'ibHezbollah-05March10.pdf (accessed October 6, 2011).

Leweling, Tara, and Ron Walters. "The Evolution of US Military Conceptions of Information Warfare and Information Operations, 1979-2004: An Initial Report."

Edited by Bill Hutchinson. *4th European Conference on Information Warfare and Security* (July 2005): 198-204.

Loi, Charles. *U.S. and Iranian Strategic Competition: Competition between the US and Iran in Iraq*. Washington, DC: Center for Strategic and International Studies, March 2, 2011. www.csis.org/Burke/studies (accessed November 20, 2011).

Wood, J. R. T. "Rethinking Counterinsurgency." *RAND Counterinsurgency Study*, Volume 5, 2008.

Personal Accounts

Clausewitz, Carl von. *On War*. Edited by Michael Howard and Peter Paret. Princeton, NJ: Princeton University Press, 1976.

Cole, Roger, and Richard Belfield. *SAS Operation Storm*. London: Hodder and Stoughton Ltd., 2010.

Galula, David. *Counterinsurgency Warfare: Theory and Practice*. London: Praeger Security International, 1964, 2006.

———. *Pacification in Algeria 1956-1958*. Santa Monica, CA: RAND, 2006.

Gardiner, Ian. *In the Service of the Sultan*. Barnsley, South Yorkshire: Pen and Sword Books Limited, 2011.

Jeapes, Tony. *SAS: Operation Oman*. London: William Kimber, 1980.

———. *SAS Secret War: Operation Storm in the Middle East*. London: Greenhill Books, 2005.

Kilcullen, David. *The Accidental Guerilla: Fighting Small Wars in the Midst of a Big One*. Oxford: Oxford University Press, 2009.

Kitson, Frank. *Bunch of Five*. London: Faber and Faber, 1977.

MacKinlay, John. *The Insurgent Archipelago*. London: C Hurst and Co. Publishers Ltd, 2009.

McCuen, John J. *The Art of Counter-Revolutionary War*. Harrisburg, PA: Stockpole Books, 1966.

Phillips, Rufus. *Why Vietnam Matters: An Eyewitness Account of Lessons Not Learned*. Annapolis, MD: Naval Institute Press, 2008.

Ray, Bryan. *Dangerous Frontiers: Campaigning in Somaliland and Oman*. Barnsley, South Yorkshire: Pen and Sword Books Limited, 2008.

Thompson, Robert. *Defeating Communist Insurgency.* London: Chatto and Windhus, 1966.

Trinquier, Roger. *Modern Warfare: A French View of Counterinsurgency.* Fort Leavenworth, KS: Combat Studies Institute, 1985.

Tse-Tung, Mao. *On Guerilla Warfare.* New York: Dover Publications, 2005.

Doctrinal References

Department of the Army. Field Manual (FM) 3-0, *Operations,* change 1. Washington, DC: Government Printing Office, February, 2011.

————. FM 3-0, *Operations.* Washington, DC: Government Printing Office,

————. FM 3-13, *Information Operations.* Washington, DC: Government Printing Office, November, 2003.

————. FM 3-13, *Information Operations (Draft).* Washington, DC: Government Prinitng Office, Unpublished.

————. FM 3-24, *Counterinsurgency.* Washington DC: Government Printing Office, 2006.

————. FM 3-90, *Tactics.* Washington, DC: Government Printing Office, January 23, 2009.

————. FM 46-1, *Public Affairs.* Washington, DC: Government Printing Office, May 30, 1997.

————. FM 100-2-1, *The Soviet Army: Operations and Tactics.* Washington, DC: Government Priniting Office. July 16, 1984.

————. FM 100-6, *Information Operations.* Washington, DC: Government Printing Office. August, 1996.

Department of Defense. Joint Publication 3-13, *Information Operations.* Washington, DC: Government Printing, 2006.

————. Joint Publication 3-61, *Public Affairs.* Washington, DC: Government Printing Office, May 9, 2005.

Secondary Sources

Books

Armistead, Leigh. *Information Warfare: Separating Hype from Reality.* Washington, DC: Potomac Books, 2007.

Beckett, Ian. "The British Counter-insurgency Campaign in Dhofar, 1965-1975." In *Counterinsurgency in Modern Warfare*, edited by Daniel Marston and Carter Malkasian, 175-190. Oxford: Osprey Publishing, 2010.

Bergerud, Eric. *The Dynamics of Defeat: The Vietnam War in Hau Nghia Province.* Oxford: Westview Press, 1991.

Cann, John P. *Counterinsurgency in Africa: The Portuguese Way of War, 1961-1974.* Westport, CT: Greenwood Press, 1997.

Cilliers, J. K. *Counter-insurgency in Rhodesia.* London: Croom Helm, 1985.

Coates, John. *Suppressing Insurgency.* Boulder, CO: Westview Press, 1992.

Comber, Leon. *Malaya's Secret Police 1945-1960: The Role of the Special Branch in the Malayan Emergency.* Melbourne: Monash University Press, 2009.

Green, T. N. *The Guerilla - Selections from the Marine Corps Gazette.* New York: Praeger.

Hammes, Thomas X. *The Sling and the Stone: On War in the 21st Century.* St. Paul, MN: Zenith Press, 2006.

Hart, Peter. *The I.R.A. at War 1916-1923.* Oxford: Oxford University Press, 2003.

Henniker, M. C. A. *Red Shadow Over Malaya.* London: William Blackwood and Sons, 1955.

Hoffman, Bruce. *Lessons for Contemporary Counterinsurgencies: The Rhodesian Experience.* Santa Monica, CA: RAND, 1992.

Hopkinson, Michael. *The Irish War of Independence.* Montreal: McGill-Queen's University Press, 2002.

Horne, Alistair. "The French Army and the Algerian War 1954-62." In *Regular Armies and Insurgency*, edited by Ronald Haycock, 69-83. London: Croom Helm, 1979.

Hunt, Richard. *Pacification: The American Struggle for Vietnam's Hearts and Minds.* Boulder, CO: Westview Press, 1995.

Iron, Richard. "Britain's Longest War: Northern Ireland 1967-2007." In *Counterinsurgency in Modern Warfare*, edited by Daniel Marston and Carter Malkasian, 157-174. Oxford: Osprey Publishing, 2010.

Jeudwine, Hugh. "A Record of the Rebellion in Ireland in 1920-1, and the Part Played by the Army in Dealing with it (Intelligence)." In *British Intelligence in Ireland: The Final Reports*, by Peter Hart, 17-60. Cork: Cork University Press, 2002.

Joes, Anthony. "Counterinsurgency in the Phillipines." In *Counterinsurgency in Modern Warfare*, edited by Daniel Marston and Carter Malkasian, 39-49. Oxford: Osprey Publishing, 2010.

Joint Forces Staff College and the National Security Agency. *Information Operations: Warfare and the Hard Reality of Soft Power*, edited by Leigh Armistead. Washington, DC: Brassey's Inc., 2004.

Komer, Robert. *Bureaucracy at War: U.S. Performance in the Vietnam Conflict.* Boulder, CO: Westview Press, 1986.

———. *The Malayan Emergency in Retrospect: Organization of a Successful Counterinsurgency Effort.* Santa Monica, CA: RAND, 1972. http://www.rand.org/pubs/reports/R957 (accessed August 6, 2011).

Krepinevich, Andrew. *The Army and Vietnam.* Baltimore, MD: Johns Hopkins University Press, 1986.

Kriger, Norma. *Zimbabwe's Guerilla War.* Cambridge: Cambridge University Press, 1993.

Linn, Brian. *The Phillipine War, 1899-1902.* Lawrence, KS: University of Kansas Press, 2000.

Malkasian, Carter. "Counterinsurgency in Iraq: May 2003-January 2010." In *Counterinsurgency in Modern Warfare*, edited by Daniel Marston and Carter Malkasian, 287-310. Oxford: Osprey Publishing, 2010.

Mansfield, Don. "The Irish Republican Army and Northern Ireland." In *Insurgency in the Modern World*, 45-86. Boulder, CO: Westview Press, 1980.

Marston, Daniel. "Lost and Found in the Jungle." In *Big Wars and Small Wars*, edited by Hew Strachan, 96-114. London: Routledge, 2006.

———. "Realizing the extent of our errors and forging the road ahead: Afghanistan 2001-2010." In *Counterinsurgency in Modern Warfare*, edited by Daniel Marston and Carter Malkasian, 251-286. Oxford: Osprey Publishing, 2010.

Marston, Daniel and Malkasian, Carter, eds.. *Counterinsurgency in Modern Warfare.* Oxford: Osprey Publishing, 2010.

Miers, Richard. *Shoot to Kill.* London: Faber and Faber, 1959.

Minford, John. *Sun Tzu The Art of War: The Essential Translation of the Classic Book of Life.* New York: Penguin Press, 2002.

Murray, Williamson, and Alan R. Millet. *Military Innovation in the Interwar Period.* New York: Cambridge University Press, 1996.

O'Neill, Bard. "Revolutionary War in Oman." In *Insurgency in the Modern World*, 213-234. Boulder, CO: Westview Press, 1980.

O'Neill, Mark. *Confronting the Hydra.* Sydney, Australia: Lowy Institute, 2009.

Paret, Peter. *French Revolutionary Warfare from Indochina to Algeria: The Analysis of a Political and Military Doctrine.* London: Pall Mall Press, 1964.

Pimlott, John. "The Algerian Revolution." In *War in Peace*, edited by Sir Robert and John Keegan Thompson, 121-135. New York: Harmony Books, 1981.

Porch, Douglas. "Bugeaud, Gallieni, Lyautey: The Development of French Colonial Warfare." In *Makers of Modern Strategy*, edited by Peter Paret, 376-407. Princeton, NJ: Princeton University Press, 1986.

———. "French Imperial Warfare 1945-62." In *Counterinsurgency in Modern Warfare*, edited by Daniel Marston and Carter Malkasian, 87-101. Oxford: Osprey Publishing, 2010.

Price, D. L. *Oman: Insurgency and Development.* London: Institute for the Study of Conflict, 1975.

Race, Jeffrey. *War Comes to Long An.* California: UC Press, 1972.

Ramsey, Robert. *Savage Wars of Peace: Case Studies of Pacification in the Philippines, 1900-1902.* Fort Leavenworth, KS: Combat Studies Institute, 2007.

Shy, John, and Thomas Collier. "Revolutionary War." In *Makers of Modern Strategy*, edited by Peter Paret, 815-862. Princeton, NJ: Princeton University Press, 1986.

Stubbs, Richard. "From Search and Destroy to Hearts and Minds: The Evolution of British Strategy in Malaya 1948-1960." In *Counterinsurgency in Modern Warfare*, edited by Daniel Marston and Carter Malkasian, 101-118. Oxford: Osprey Publishing, 2010.

Sutherland, Riley. *Army Operations in Malaya, 1947-1960.* Santa Monica, CA: RAND, 1964.

Thompson, W. Scott, and Donaldson Frizzell. *The Lessons of Vietnam.* New York: Crane, Russak and Company, 1977.

Townshend, Charles. "In Aid of the Civil Power." In *Counterinsurgency in Modern Warfare*, edited by Daniel Marston and Carter Malkasian, 21-31. Oxford: Osprey Publishing, 2010.

Ucko, David. *The New Counterinsurgency Era: Transforming the US Military for Modern Wars.* Washington, DC: Georgetown University Press, 2009.

Warren, Charlie. *Stick Leader: RLI.* South Africa: Just Done Productions, 2007.

Willbanks, James. *Abandoning Vietnam.* Lawrence, KS: University of Kansas Press, 2004.

Wood, J. R. T. "Countering the CHIMURENGA: The Rhodesian Counterinsurgency Campaign." In *Counterinsurgency in Modern Warfare*, edited by Daniel Marston and Carter Malkasian, 191-208. Oxford: Osprey Publishing, 2010.

———. *Counterstrike From the Sky: The Rhodesian All-Arms Fireforce in the War in the Bush 1974-1980.* South Africa: 30 Degrees South Publishers, 2009.

Periodicals

Afsar, Shahid, and Chris Samples. "The Taliban: An organizational analysis." *Military Review* (May-June 2008): 58-73.

Al-Jabouri, Najim Abed, and Sterling Jensen. "The Iraqi and AQI roles in the Sunni Awakening." *Prism* 2, no. 1 (December 2010): 1-16.

Andrade, Dale. "Westmoreland was right: Learning the wrong lessons from the Vietman War." *Small Wars and Insurgencies* 19, no. 2 (June 2008): 145-181.

Bamford, Bradley. "The role and effectiveness of Intelligence in Northern Ireland." *Intelligence and National Security* 20, no. 4 (December 2005): 581-607.

Barno, David. "Fighting the other war: Counterinsurgency strategy in Afghanistan 2003-2005." *Military Review* (September-October 2007): 32-44.

Boyd, Curtis D. "Army IO is PSYOP: Influencing more with less." *Military Review* (May-June 2007): 67-75.

Burton, Brian, and John Nagl. "Learning as we go: The US Army adapts to COIN in Iraq." *Small Wars and Insurgencies* 19, no. 3 (September 2008): 303-327.

Chiarelli, Pete, and Patrick Michaelis. "The Requirements for Full-Spectrum Operations." *Military Review* 85, no. 4 (July-August 2005): 4-17.

Collier, Craig. "Now that we're leaving Iraq, what did we learn." *Military Review* (September-October 2010): 88-93.

Gentile, Gian. "A strategy of tactics: Population centric COIN and the Army." *Parameters* (Autumn 2009): 5-17.

Hack, Karl. "The Malayan Emergency as a Counter-Insurgency Paradigm." *The Journal of Strategic Studies* 32, no. 3 (June 2009): 383-414.

Hoffman, Frank G. "Hybrid Warfare and Challenges." *Joint Forces Quarterly* (1st Quarter, 2009): 34-39.

———. "Neo-Classical Counterinsurgency?" *Parameters* (Summer 2007): 71-87.

Johnson, Thomas, and M. Chris Mason. "No Sign until the Burst of Fire: Understanding the Pakistan-Afghanistan Frontier." *International Security* 32, no. 4 (Spring 2008).

Ladwig, Walter, III. "Supporting Allies in COIN: Britain and the Dhofar Rebellion." *Small Wars and Insurgencies* 19, no. 1 (March 2008): 62-88.

Malkasian, Carter. "The Role of Perceptions and Political reform in Counterinsurgency: The Case of Western Iraq, 2004-2005." *Small Wars and Insurgencies* 17, no. 3 (September 2006): 367-394.

Marston, Daniel. "Adaptation in the Field: The British Army's Difficult Campaign in Iraq." *Security Challenges* 6, no. 1 (Autumn 2010).

———. "The Indian Army, Partition, and the Punjab Boundary Force, 1945-1947." *War in History* 4, no. 15 (2009): 469-505.

McCuen, John J. "Hybrid Wars." *Military Review* (March-April 2008): 107-113.

Metz, Steve. "New Challenges and Old Concepts: Understanding 21st Century Insurgency." *Parameters* (Summer 2010).

Omrani, Bijan. "The Durand Line: History and Problems of the Afghan-Pakistan Border." *Asian Affairs* 40, no. 2 (2009).

Rubin, Barnett, and Ahmed Rashid. "The Great Game to the Great Bargain." *Foreign Affairs* 87, no. 6 (November-December 2008): 30-44.

Smith, Simon. "General Templer and Counter-insurgency in Malaya: Hearts and Minds, intelligence, and propaganda." *Intelligence and National Security* 16, no. 3 (June 2010): 60-78.

Thornton, Rod. "Getting it wrong: The crucial mistakes made in the early stages of the British Army's deployment to Northern Ireland." *Journal of Strategic Studies* 30, no. 1 (February 2007): 72-107.

Townshend, Charles. "The IRA and the Development of Guerilla Warfare." *English Historical Review* 94 (April 1979): 318-345.

Tripodi, Christian. "Good for one but not the other: The Sandeman System of Pacification as Applied to Baluchistan and the North-West Frontier, 1877-1947." *The Journal of Military History* 73, no. 3 (July 2009).

Web Resources

Corum, James. "Training Indigenous Forces in Counterinsurgency: A Tale of Two Insurgencies." March 2006. http://www.strategicstudiesinstitute.army.mil/pubs/display.cfm?PubID=648(accessed August 15, 2011).

Foreign Policy Research Institute. *Lieutenant Colonel Frank Hoffman.* www.fpri.org/about/people/hoggman.html (accessed November 6, 2011).

Glenn, Russell W. "Thoughts on 'Hybrid' Conflict." *Small Wars Journal*, March 2009. http://www.smallwarsjournal.com (accessed August 15, 2011).

Hoffman, Frank G. "Further Thoughts on Hybrid Threats." *Small Wars Journal*, 2009. www.smallwarsjournal.com (accessed August 15, 2011).

————. "Hybrid vs. Compound War." *Armed Forces Journal*, October 2009. www.armedforcesjournal.com/2009 (accessed August 15, 2011).

Public Affairs Office, United States Forces-Iraq. "ISF campaigns against Kata'ib Hezbollah weapons smuggling, rocket-attack network along Iraq-Iran border." *United States Forces-Iraq.* February 12, 2010. www.USF-Iraq.com/news/press-releases (accessed October 6, 2011).

Roggio, Bill. "The Long War Journal: Iranian-backed Shia terror group remains a threat in Iraq: General Odierno." *The Long War Journal.* July 13, 2010. www.longwarjournal.org/archives/2010/07/iranianbacked_shia_t_1.php (accessed October 6, 2011).

Weinberger, Casper. *PBS.org Frontline.* November 28, 1984. http://pbs.org/wgbh/pages/frontline/shows/military/force/weinberger.html (accessed August 18, 2011).

Other Sources

Alderson, Alexander. "The Validity of British Army Counterinsurgency Doctrine after the War in Iraq 2003-2009." PhD diss., Cranfield University, 2010.

O'Connor, Patrick. *Iraq: US military raid on Iranian-backed terrorist organization.* The Global Realm. http://theglobalrealm.com/2010/02/15/iraq-us-military-raid-on-%E2%80%9Ciranian-backed-terrorist-organisation%E2%80%9D/ (accessed November 23, 2011).

Salman, Raheem. "Iraqi cleric calls halt to attacks on US troops." *The Los Angeles Times*, September 12, 2011. http://articles.latimes.com/2011/sep/12/world/la-fg-iraq-sadr-20110912 (accessed November 23, 2011).